For Papa

A coming of age story

*Dedicated to Gajinderpal Singh Sahni, beloved
and extraordinary girl's dad*

By

Harleen Sahni

Dedication

Thank you, Papa

"Koee bhee kaam chhota ya bada nahin hota"

"No job is big or small" - Papa

Papa was born into a family where there wasn't much love given to him. Rav told me a story that Papa told her when he started getting sick in 2020. Papa said how when he was a child, he had fallen from the roof of his house in India. Papa was hurt, but his parents didn't take him to the hospital but to rest in he bed. Papa was sick and these were things he was remembering. I agree that my grandparents and my aunt and uncles had no love for my Papa because, as a child and adult, I saw how they saw and treated my father. They felt he was a loser, and therefore, my sisters and I were put under the same label. However, I feel my Papa's life transformed when he married my mother. My loving mother transformed my Papa's life. As a child, I went to Macy's with my mom, and she would buy clothes for my father. It was a surprise to learn from my mother that when she married my father, he only carried two shirts. It was a surprise because I always saw my father dressed to the nine. Tailored pants, pressed button-down shirts, wool coats, and trench coats to match the season. My mother is also very social, and when my parents settled in New York City, my mother easily and quickly made friends.

She made a circle and society. My parents were very socially active people. They went to their social events on the weekends and wouldn't miss a party even if they had to drive from Connecticut. As a child, watching them get dressed for their parties was a production. All the bathrooms were occupied. My mother told my sisters and me about how she would push my father to do what he wanted. Even the simple things like wanting to go out to eat lunch at the corner restaurant. I remember my mom saying with emotion about my father expressing how he feels like eating out, and my

i

mother would just say to my father if your heart is set on it, then go like, why are you stopping yourself?

My mother didn't understand that, and it upset her because she grew up in a home where she was encouraged to express what she wanted and got it, but my father didn't. My mother wanted my father to look good and feel good. With the clothes, the friends, parties at very nice places, and with the love, my mother transformed my father's live. I believe it came as a surprise to my father because I don't think he was expecting that when he married my mother. Knowing how my father's own parents and siblings saw and treated him, I don't think my father expected that. To go from two shirts to a lot of nice clothes, to have friends who lived in the very nice towns of Long Island, parties in nice places, but most important, the love from my mother, my sisters, and I. I believe the life my father created with my mother was far greater than the one he had as a child. So, I do believe that God dreams a bigger dream for you than you can ever for yourself. In knowing that I feel that it's okay that one can't choose what family they are born into because it's not the end of all. But it's not so much the material stuff that matters. Love is what matters.

My father received a lot of love from my mother, my sisters, all the dogs, and me. When my father was sick, we all took care of him. Especially my mom. She became a nurse. She remained strong and positive, continued cooking for my father, continued to be encouraging to my father, and cared for him up until the end. My sisters and I agreed that not everyone is so lucky to get that kind of love from a partner, a spouse, or a family. After my father passed away, my mother would put money in my father's pant pockets. My mother said she did it so my father's pockets weren't empty. I believe my father's heart was full of all the love.

Growing up, early Sunday mornings, I would be in bed, and the curtains were closed in the condominium of Bayside, Queens. Papa would enter my room and open the curtains to let the sun in. He would gently say wake up in Hindi. I wouldn't want to get up since it was Sunday morning. However, Papa would say we have to go to gurdwara (temple). Then, he would eloquently talk about how we have a religion, and we have this day to give thanks. There were many moments where Papa would have to give me the conversation. Mornings, when I didn't feel like going to school, he would say if you get up, take a shower, and you will feel refreshed. Papa never screamed or shouted. It was always a warm and gentle tone. I never saw Papa sleep in, even on the weekends. He was diligent and punctual about waking up in the morning to start the day. I remember being home after school, and Papa had just come back from the airport on his business trip to the Caribbean or Virgin Islands. He came into the room with his long trench coat while I was playing with Barbies. Papa put his suit case down and went to grab his briefcase to head to the city. Now going to the city meant taking the bus to the subway, so for Papa to do that after landing from a long trip reflected his work ethic.

My sisters and I saw Papa work hard first-hand. Even when we went to his office in Manhattan, where he was very strict and focused on work. We were not to bother him, and he was not in Papa mode at his office. Yet, we saw Papa's business have downs, which became hard to bounce back from. Initially, Papa sold ivory, but then it got banned in the states. Then he went into diamonds and precious stones. The office was lost, yet Papa went to the city to do business. When there was no business, Papa took a goods delivery job for 99-cent stores. He didn't see any job as big or small. He was active and the jobs he did required physicality. Papa never stopped. To do physical jobs in your 60s and go into the city. Papa worked until the end. It's like that saying, "dying with your boots on." Papa wanted it that way. I remember the pandemic, everything shut down, and people were required to stay home. Papa didn't like that. He was worried about his business and wanted to work. A friend of his said to him that this is the time to relax and rest. Papa responded this is too much rest and relax. It was also around this time that Papa started showing symptoms. Yet, he was a strong and hard-working man.

We also saw Papa seek our Ma as a business partner. When we went to Atlantic City, and Papa went to his clients, we sat at the bench with Ma until Papa returned. We would kill time by eating the soft serve ice cream, funnel cake, roasted peanuts, or popcorn that was sold on the boardwalk. I remember my parent's conversations. Papa would return and discuss with Ma about his business clients. Ma would give her suggestions. I just remember how Papa would ask us when a client was not here, "Hor Koi Kaam Nai Hai, so chalho," (There is no one else I need to meet so we can go). Then Ma would be firm and suggest that we, the kids, can ghum or see things. Papa would then reiterate there is no kham here, but if you want to stay so, the kids can ghum or vacation. In those moments, Ma would get frustrated. Papa would like to have long conversations, and Ma would be impatient, like get to the point or what do you want to do. Ma would say "Ab kya karna hai?" (What do you want to do now?).

Thank you, Papa, for being brave to leave your home in India, where everything was set and come to establish a life in America. You pursued your goals with many trips to America while Ma, Simran and Raveena were in India. Thank you, Papa, for being the best male figure in your daughter's life through how you carried yourself. Papa, you were our go to person and who we would consult with and seek guidance. The greatest quality of my father was that he was curious and would ask to know how things went in our daily lives. I remember when I returned from parent teacher conferences at night from when I taught in Whitestone. I came home, and Papa was the first person I saw sitting at the dining table in the kitchen. Papa pointed out what a long day I had and asked if I had conferences all day. Then I would explain to him how it works with the half day. Finally, my father would ask how it was and if there were a lot of parents. I would say "Aacha ta aaj" (Today was good).

No one has control over where and who they are born into. Many people are born in really worst situations. Then, when you are an adult, it is your responsibility to change the narrative and make life the way you wish or desire. With me, I held onto the anger and became angry. To make it worse for myself, I didn't have the courage or confidence to change my narrative. To go get the life I wanted and be happy. I was 36 when my father passed away, and I lived with him for all those years. I know my father. I observed and worshiped my father. After he passed away, I surrounded myself with who he was. I did what he did. My father listened to hymns, so I did. I woke up to those sounds because he listened to them while praying. My father was a temple goer, so I went to the temple. It was part of the grieving. When you lose someone that dear and close, you try to feel their presence by surrounding yourself with their joys, I couldn't turn to my father to help me with the hurt, so I turned to what gave him joy. That was who he was. His identity.

During the three years after my father passed, I listened to Sikh hymns. Sometimes, when driving to work, exercising, or just casually doing nothing, When I listen to Papa's favorite hymn or Shabad, it is like time traveling to another world. The most recent memory I have is the living room in the Glen Oaks house. Papa's face, red shirt and the little holy book in his hands as he prays with a towel or shawl on his head. It brings a smile to my face, and I needed to listen to the hymns when Papa was sick or in the hospital when I was trying to do normal things like go to work, do the treadmill, or teach remotely. I needed to hear the hymns after Papa passed to lessen the anger. I feel honored and truly treasure knowing that I witnessed/saw in front of me an incredible man who I called my father.

Papa was a gentleman and team player. As a family, there were times we had to share a room if the air conditioner stopped working or the new bedroom furniture didn't arrive. Papa, always volunteered to sleep on the floor and give us women the bed. One time, Ma's relatives came, and Rav, Cole, and I had to sleep in one room. We were in our thirties, and Papa came to check on us and we started gossiping about how Ma's relatives lost their passport to be stuck here. Papa said they were idiots to be walking around with their passports. They should put it in a secure place. We started laughing, and I would get loud. Rav would say, whisper to me. Papa would immediately whisper and speak in a low, slow tone to show me how it was done. Other people felt Papa was quiet but not with us. Papa, you were and still are vibrant.

You are also responsible for making your life sweet. When my Papa started showing signs of being sick, my life wasn't sweet, and I was angry. I was in a toxic school, administrators felt I wasn't doing anything, and I felt like I sucked as a teacher. I feel finding a cockroach in my hair after using the bathroom on my first day at the school was a foreshadowing sign. This job was my whole focus besides my immediate family. When you are angry, you can't love. I was mean to my father, and I yelled at him.

The universe is controlled by love and love alone. Outside love's embrace, the world is chaos. Growing up, my father's love was the embrace that kept our family together despite the chaos that was the result of having no money. Losing Papa was losing the embrace, and the world became chaotic and you see that there are unkind people out there who don't care about what you are going through. Then you indulge in the thought that if only we were somewhere else, things would be better is a surefire way to experience pain.

When Papa passed away, I felt it was unfair. However, the situation Rav, Sim, and I were in due to the financial difficulties was unfair. That whole time, the focus was on the financial problems. We didn't focus on ourselves and carving each of our individual lives. Rav having to end up paying for and taking care of the whole family was unfair. Knowing all that occurred made it difficult to make sense of losing my father. It made the grieving harder and longer because I couldn't make peace, sense of it, or have the answers. I believe fairness is up to God and Babaji. Don't question what is fair. Leave it to God to do and make things fair.

Papa, you helped me every step of the way towards becoming a teacher. Papa, I know when you were sick you questioned if you were successful and if you accomplished things. Papa, even with the fights, we never thought you would leave us when you did. So suddenly. We never wanted that. You wondered if it was bad wishes that got you sick because there were people who thought you made bad choices or did wrong by the kids. I know your brother, your sister, and your parents made you feel that you weren't successful. With this book, I want you to see and feel from where you are that you are successful. Papa, your life and story have reached an audience and is well-known.

Papa, you expressed not feeling well in March 2020. Literally, came into the room where Sim, Rav, and I were to tell us. We were trying to figure out what was wrong and why you were losing weight. You only got weaker and thinner. It was December when you went to the hospital the last time. You were on oxygen, and the paramedics decided to take you off just until you got into the ambulance.

However, you lost consciousness, and they had to call a doctor to come and resuscitate you. When you got to the hospital, the doctors called and said the CO_2 had filled the lungs and to let you go. But we wanted to give you a chance and said to put you on the ventilator. The doctors said that you won't get off of it. However, Papa got off the ventilator, and that is when you wrote Rav's cell number on the paper. We couldn't see you because of COVID restrictions, and we would call the hospital. They would tell us to call back because they had to go find an iPad. The last time I saw you, Papa, was on an iPad. Rav and Sim got to see you at the hospital. However, I think about that last summer that you were with us, Papa. Papa, always did nightly prayers with the holy book (Guru Granth Saab).

One night during that summer, I was sitting in the living room, and Papa was near me praying with his holy book. When he finished, Papa would close the holy book have it between his palms, and bow (mata). That night, Papa did something different. Even though I was looking at my cell phone, I would look up and take glances at Papa praying. That night, he closed the holy book and, holding the holy book between his palms, he turned towards me and bowed (took mata) towards me. I don't know why Papa did that. I didn't ask and should have asked. I think Papa had me in his prayers like he always did, but he really wanted Babaji, God, to watch over me.

There is a saying or line in a Bollywood movie. The line is that our lives are just like movies in the sense that, in the end, everything is okay and good. If it's not okay and good, then it's not the end. At the end of my father's life, everything was okay and good. Papa saw my nephew and his grandson Jordan enter the world. Papa saw Simran living with us for a year until she went back to California with her husband. Papa saw me skinny. I lost weight, and he saw me teaching. However, I wasn't happy at the school I was teaching in at that time. I was having a hard time. The higher-ups or administration were not happy with my performance. I would come home to complain and cry. Papa would console me, and he said you be strong and show them. I thought those words were just for the moment. I was wrong. After Papa passed away, I was let go from that school. I taught in other schools. One year here and another year somewhere else.

Those words of my father have been universal for me as I navigate life. Be strong and show them what you are made of, but also show yourself what you are made of. It is important because when you embrace what you resist, then you can see yourself from the bigger power.

What I know is true is that there are crappie people in this world. More crappie than good. Yet if you are good in heart and true to who you are then you can never go wrong. My father passed away unexpectedly and sooner than I should have. Yet, in his 72 years and 44 years as a father, he left us with his philosophical sayings. He prepared us to deal with and face life without him. When I worked as a cashier, I got upset because I got written up for giving the wrong change amount to a customer. He was Asian and took it. My father picked me up that evening from work and told me that just because one did it doesn't mean they are all like that.

To make me feel better Sim and Ma would echo the same point. What is really gone? When a loved one passes, are they really gone? They reassured me that a loved one is always with us. Papa is here and with me. Even Jess, the astrologer, said your father is guiding you every step of the way. He is more powerful now than ever. Before Papa passed away, my prayers were I don't know what is to happen in my life, but you know God.

After Papa passed away, I felt someone I consider my own had gone to God and Babaji. Papa was one of our own, part of our clan and tribe. He saw what we as a family struggled with as a unit and our individual struggles. Papa saw first hand. So, Papa knows what we want and our dreams. He is in a powerful position to make them happen for us. What Papa couldn't do here, he can do where he is because he is next to God and Babaji.

Every parent does to their best ability. I don't have complaints because I know Papa did, but he, like every parent, has their karma and demons.

I remember going to a wedding with Papa. I was in college, and he met these two ladies from the bride's side. He introduced me and said she was going to be in Hollywood. She is going to write stories. Papa already envisioned this for me.

When I was scared to drive, Papa said to Ma that perhaps I would be in a place where I wouldn't need to know how to drive. That I will be driven. Papa saw greatness in everything I did, even when I didn't. When of my dearest memories is when I drove to my first school as a teacher. My dad was with me when I went for the interview in Whitestone, Queens, and he commented that it's a nice neighborhood. My first day at that middle school in Whitestone, Queens, fell on the same day as Papa's birthday. During the six years I taught there, Papa passed away in my 5th year there. Yet, when I got that teaching job it was instant and fell into my path easily.

I dedicate this book to someone who was extraordinary, mature, connected to God, intuitive, someone who possessed the life lessons to raise me, and someone who gave it his all to make my life sweet. Papa, you are in all my classrooms, reminding me to show them, serve, and do good work.

Acknowledgment

My Papa's picture reminds me of my foundation. There is a huge picture of my father above the fireplace, and there is a painted portrait of my father in the dining area. I look at it and I know where I came from. Growing up, there was a lot of ups and downs due to financial issues. I remember growing up, and the electricity would be cut, or the cable would be cut, or the car would get repossessed. My sisters and I would joke that it was a good day when nothing was cut or taken. Even though there were a lot of problems, I was part of a family where there was a lot of love. We loved each other and took care of each other. I, being the youngest, was protected. I would say protected in the sense that I knew what was going on but the repercussions weren't so heavy when I went to school or outside. It didn't seem to impact me on the outside if anyone saw me.

Little Harleen grew up going with her parents to their friend's homes and playing with their kids on the weekends. In Hindi, it was called the kitty parties. As the years went by, the kids got married and had kids. It was hard to feel like the outcast who wasn't there yet. Also, at the workplace seeing women my age already "set." It was very hard because of the judgment I held for myself I thought others bestowed as well. What I know is that every culture and society does whisper the checkpoints of when to do what. From what I saw with my elder sisters and my own life is making your own checkpoints. Pave your own way.

What I mean is when I was in 7th grade, my parents couldn't take me to buy new clothes for back to school. There was no money for that, and what happened? My two older sisters, who worked as part-time cashiers, took me to buy clothes. I remember Simran, who was 21 took me to buy jeans at Express. Raveena took me to buy tops and went to our Dad to let him know all I need are new shoes. She got money from our Dad, and I was in the other room. I remember her saying, "Harleen, let's go. I got money for your shoes." I get emotional every time I write about that moment. Who does that?

So far, in all my years, I haven't met better people like my sisters. Even if I saw a glimpse of that in someone then they quickly reverted. I ask who does that. Better people do that. Now I know a lot of siblings care and love each other. I know my sisters love me, and I love them. That was the basis of why they did what they did for me. But what they did was so beyond, and it is an example that better means to care. To care and really put yourself in another person's shoes. Not everyone has that ability. It is really profound and an example of the great upbringing of my parents to instill that ability. At 21 and 18 my sisters cared enough and understood how it would make me feel not to be wearing new clothes on the first day of school. They didn't want the problems to affect how I carried myself out into the world. So they protected me. People talk of guardian angels who guard from above. I wrote this when I was 5 in a diary, that my guardian angels are here next to me in the physical sense. My two older sisters are my guardian angels. I have held on to everything they say and their experiences. I also once wrote that my sisters have fulfilled every role every person needs in their life, and growing up they did that for me. If you are lucky, the better people in your life will be the people in your family.

Now, for some, that is not the case, and I have seen that. I remember when I worked as a middle school ENL teacher in Queens. The school was in a rich area, but the school had kids from low-income families because they bused kids from all over. My ENL students were immigrants, migrants, and poor. I had students who, unfortunately didn't have the better people as their family members. I saw them, and they didn't know English. Some wore the same shirt every day, and from relating my personal experiences, I gravitated to serving kids based on wanting them to feel not different or less. Early on it was giving goody bags with candy for every holiday. Teach them with the best lesson plans I can and talk to their families. Find out where they come from and their culture. I was really pulled when I saw and heard the things they were going through. As a teacher I got personally invested and would go beyond to get what they needed.

That was letting the guidance counselor know that this student needed to talk to someone. Or during the COVID pandemic, when a student of mine, John, messaged me online, "Ms. Sahni, I have problems in my house." That would get me personally invested as a teacher, and I immediately responded from just that line with the words "problems" and "house" because growing up, there were problems in my house.

I immediately emailed the guidance counselor at 10 pm. I called his house the next day and found out they didn't have WiFi to get online. I emailed the Assistant Principal and asked if the city offered WiFi in these situations. I knew how it felt when someone goes up and beyond for you, so I wanted to do these things for my students. It came naturally to me. I also feel teaching in that middle school and teaching kids at an early age provided perspective and closure. Growing up with the problems of electricity, cable and cars being repossessed and seeing my students going through the same problems but not being able to excel in academics makes me know that I was fortunate.

I was because I had a family that put my focus in the right place, which was on education and grades. I was in a culture where how you academically was where the spotlight was. I didn't go down the wrong path or end up hanging out with the wrong people. I got a job as a cashier at 18 years old, but I still kept good grades and was in AP classes.

When I decided to write this book, it was something my older sister Simran suggested after I expressed that I really wanted to get my writing out there.

It was during the summer after I completed the leave replacement teacher position at a school near where I lived. During the summer, I was applying and interviewing for teaching positions, but nothing close to home or in Queens was coming through.

Then, my sister suggested unemployment, and I could tutor in the afternoons. September came, and Raveena had to go to court for work on Jordan's first day of Pre-K. I was home, and I took Jordan with my gym clothes on since I was going to head to the gym afterward. He was nervous while I was holding his hand and walking to the school.

There is a red floored ramp, and as we are walking over it, I can see Jordan is wondering what is going on. It reminded me of when Papa would drop me off at school. Holding my hand as we walked to the elementary school.

The universe listens to your intentions and provides opportunities. Raveena was leaning towards an opportunity to work at a firm that would pay more, but she had to go to Manhattan three days a week. I expressed my intention that I could drop Jordan off at school since I was home.

Then Raveena expressed her intention that she needs help with Jordan when I get a job. Then, I expressed my intention of having these few months as my time.

Then Raveena expressed the intention of me dropping Jordan to school, going to the gym and enjoying this time since you have worked hard all these years with no break.

I am thinking how these past three years, with all that occurred I didn't give myself one to heal. Through all those expressed intentions came the opportunity. Sometimes that doesn't happen. One of Raveena's intentions when Jordan was born was that Papa and Ma would drop Jordan at school and pick him up. She knew for sure that Papa would help with Jordan since Papa would drive to Target in Elmont to get his formula.

That didn't happen. I see it as an opportunity when I am driving Jordan to Pre-K or when I would pick him up from nursery on my lunch break while I am working the leave replacement. It is an opportunity for me to give back some of the support Raveena has given me.

It is an opportunity to do what Papa would have done if he was still here with us in the physical. It's in his shoes when I do that and even when I take Ma to her doctor appointments or physical therapy. Perhaps all that happened on the job front was to give me the opportunity. I have tremendous acknowledgment and gratitude to my Papa, my sisters Simran and Raveena, my Ma, our first dog Lucky, our second dog Cole, my nephew Jordan, and now our third dog Andy.

About the Author

Writing was my outlet and escape. I remember growing up and being the one in my room with a pen & notebook. I have numerous journals that represent my years growing up. When there were financial problems, I wrote. When my best friends in high school stopped talking to me, I wrote. After learning that my dad passed away, I wrote. I couldn't express myself through voice, so writing allowed me to express all my feelings inside.

A lot of people believe we learn and develop certain skills due to our experiences. I don't believe that. I feel this ability to write comes from God. He put this skill in me, and the universe presented me with the experiences to use it as a way to escape/cope, so writing became a passion. I believe talent and where God places you goin talent and where God places you hand in hand. Now, we can't choose where and what we are born to. I don't negatively mean that at all. God put me in a powerful position because God gave me the ability to write.

Experiences allowed me to use it to cope, and it became my passion. I saw myself as a writer, and God did something even better. As a writer, I didn't have to create or look for stories. God put me in a powerful position, an extraordinary position, where I looked at the experiences of my parents and two older sisters. Those became my stories. Extraordinary people, extraordinary experiences, and extraordinary experiences, and I was a first-hand witness. I am thankful to God for placing me where he did. Having two older sisters who I see as angels. They fulfilled every role every person needs in every phase of life growing up..

When my best friends stopped talking to me, my sisters became my best friends. When my parents didn't have enough money to buy me clothes for school, my sisters stepped in. They only worked part-time jobs as cashiers and went to school.

Growing up, one thing I was certain of was, I was certain that I grew up in an extraordinary family. Saw my dad fight many obstacles; my mom, my two older sisters, and I were a unit that overcame a lot.

If I have demonstrated any fighting ability or strength, it's because I saw it and learned it from them. I learned from the best. I have always been a dreamer. As a kid not want to be normal but famous. I felt being an actress would get me there. Then, I got into writing and journalism.

Imagining that would get me there, the dreamer in me imagined being with & married to celebrities or famous people that I had crushes on at the time. But then you have to be real. I started dreaming of wanting to be married to guys associated with Ma's circle. It didn't work out, and I feel that is your way of saying telling Babaji and God not to let go of that original dream or stop being the big dreamer. Dreams are imagining being somewhere far beyond where you are in reality. Perhaps that is why I feel I don't fit in LHS167 because I am a dreamer.

Dreaming of being with Daniel but being interested in him is far beyond what I imagined for myself. Prior to that, I had imagined marrying a son of my mom's friend or mom's relative. I felt that made sense and was practical for me since I wasn't out-dating or looking for anyone different. I thought it was practical to look through my mom and her circle.

Then I saw Daniel's profile. Babaji & God, on an app. It opened something in me, the dreamer. I found myself back as that kid who dreamed of being somewhere far beyond where I really was. The idea of living with a boyfriend and being with someone not affiliated with my mom is a dream I have never had. It was magical when I sent that wave, and you liked it with a heart emoji.

A fairy-tale. I asked Daniel what a stress x-ray was on the day Papa went to the hospital, and he responded. Then I said it sounded painful, and he said it's it was only 10 seconds. When I saw his video on YouTube for showing Q&A with interested medical students, I saw it showing Q&A with interested medical students. I saw that he used the same stress x-ray.

He also pointed out it's uncomfortable, but it takes 10 seconds, and that connection/synchronicity of him pointing out something I asked was magical for me, Babaji & God. It was like a story that was playing out, which the universe wrote.

Table of Contents

It's intuition, foreshadowing, or deep connection that allows one to sense a change in the other person. I called out from work on Monday and was looking for a tote to put on clothes that do not fit me or are for fall. I went to the two totes that had sun shoes and emptied one. I found a paper with revealing news. I got hurt because of the dysfunction, and that pattern reappears again.

I get angry at Mami because if I were a mother, then I wouldn't want my daughter to do things in secrecy; I would want her to share her wants with me. By snooping it, I found out my older sister had a boyfriend in high school. I cried because why can't normal things be out there and in the air? Why does it have to be hidden from our parents?

So this week, I thought of my older sister, and it was just random thoughts at night while going to sleep; I would remember/reminisce about how Rav was when I was in college. I was working in Eckerd, and she would come in. She was skinny and looked younger than me. She was vibrant, assertive, and a go-getter. Seeing her bloom and do the things has been a treasure in my life. I told Mami to stop stressing her and not make her pay for the food at your kitty. Mami said Papa is going to give half and just knowing how that has manifested in the past (Rav paying for the people they didn't give food in triplex and getting no money). I asked Mami, "What is the point of this kitty?" Thinking in my head, *how do they even relate now since their friends' kids are married and they have grandkids?* This is all foreshadowing irony, a sense of what will be revealed to me today. Ma said that she couldn't do anything, which answers everything.

1

So today, when our parents were out for the grocery shopping, I told Rav about the clear blue directions. I joked that I knew it wasn't hers. I told her it belonged to Sun, and she took it when she was here. I joked that maybe the previous person who lived here 6 years ago asked why you were bothered by that since she said that she wanted to have a kid. I said I was bothered that she hid and did it in secrecy. She takes it by herself when she has someone. We were talking about Sun and her getting stuck because she depends on this guy.

Then I switched gears to Rav that you shouldn't be stuck and have the things you want. Rav got emotional and said it was an expiration date for what she wanted. The things she wanted have reached an expiration date. I got emotional and gave an example of a woman having a kid at 40. Then she said I know how to speak the truth indirectly. She said; First, I meet someone at 40, then a year later, we get married, and then another year, have a kid. I told her she could have the kid first. Another foreshadowing and irony of what the truth is. Also, that comment comforted her ability to tell me at that moment. Rav said she was having a baby. I said when, and she said August. Rav told me all her work friends knew, and they gave her all this. Then she took me upstairs, and she took out from the back of her closet (hiding) all this baby stuff.

Then, in a natural moment or naturally, we scattered all the stuff on the spare bed. Rav and I were talking about the stuff. It was so raw, and I told Rav you can throw this bed out because she wants to make it a nursery. She said there was more stuff in her car trunk, and I took it out, where I found a bag from her friend (work) Irene. It said Sahni baby/baby Sahni. Seeing that felt wonderful, and when I went upstairs to Babaji's picture, I cried happily and said, "Thank you, Babaji!"

I know Rav wanted this, which is why it came up because I remember perhaps ten years ago when she vented to me and Sim, too. She said that she wanted to have a family and it all. We talked about Mami and Papa, and I said she shouldn't get dramatic. That's when I got emotional. Talking emotionally and then stopping to hold it together for Rav, starting a sentence and ending in a verge tears voice. It's emotional to think Rav was keeping this in and hiding the baby stuff. It's that hiding and secrecy. It just reminds me that Mami is the mother she is. In some ways, she failed as a mother when she said she couldn't do anything for her daughters.

In a way, I had the intuition, and Babaji prepared me. Rav is a leader, and how progressive she is has been revealed. To my surprise, it is slightly bold. However, she is brave and strong in her choice. That doesn't surprise me; Rav has always been strong and brave.

The universe and situations have prepared her for this. I am going to be an aunt to a boy nephew. It is a blessing/miracle that I didn't think. Rav was right; you shouldn't give up on your wants and the things you want.

Babaji, I trust you, and you always have to give me what I am meant for and meant to be. I am just hung up on Gavin/Navjot Singh. My thoughts and wishes for him have surpassed the limits of the previous two. I was told he has a girlfriend, and that sucks, but still, I am hung up. I know I am doing this all to myself and thinking of and being hung up on someone who isn't even in front of me, who I haven't met but saw pictures of. But what can I do, Babaji? I can't help my feelings going towards what I get attracted to and hung up on.

My attraction went to him, and so did my feelings and the thoughts I created. It went to this person with status, somewhat in society. Is it wrong to want that? I don't think I was really thinking of the status stuff, but more of him. If I were, I would have just gone to Jas's daughter's wedding with Mom. I didn't let my mom. I requested my mom not to go. Perhaps that is why I had to end up hearing that he has a girlfriend. I want it to go in my favor. Then I think of kismet and chances.

Was the opportunity then and not now, when it was her wedding, and I could have met him then? I can't believe that in my heart. Timing is when it's your time, and it can't be that it was then the moment to connect with him and not now. Babaji, all I know is I am hung up on this guy and let me be clear: it's a want I am expressing. I wasn't hung up on him then (I don't know why), but I am hung up and (want him) now. For some reason, I just got these emotions and feelings. It's all intertwined, and I don't know what my kismet is.

Are you sure about that? OUT

Thinking of scenes to fulfill some content or to feel better about where I am. Last Sunday, Ma told me Sonam was having a baby. Then, after a few minutes, I was bawling my eyes out and venting to my parents about how I felt stuck and the solo situation with Morris not wanting to give me tenure or an extension. The things she said just woke me up. I said to my parents that the things I want or when I express what I want, I don't get. When I told Mom about Jaspreet's son-in-law's brother, she told Mom he had a girlfriend.

It's been these disappointments, and then I let go that perhaps I don't get these things and that I am destined for something else. I am angry, but perhaps all this is for the best. A few minutes later, Rav asked if I had heard of Kobe Brentt. Then I turned the news on, and he passed in a helicopter crash. His 13-year-old daughter was with him and other family friends. Then I think of the short life but fulfilled with the dreams coming true. Yet that I am 35, I am more confused than ever and feel stuck. I am not saying Whitestone would suck; I am okay to leave and have a change, Babaji, you know.

Babaji. If I am still dreaming and in my dreams is a life totally different than the one I am leading, then I have to be honest with myself that what I am doing right now is not my passion. This is my response to Rav's question about teaching my passion. Being on this mid-winter break and everything regarding the tenure, extension, and Morris. Babaji, this is my response that I still dream and have dreams of things that don't align with the life I am leading. Babaji, I want to dream and have those dreams come true. I don't want anything to take away from that or that away.

5

There is a pandemic around the world, and schools have been closed since 03/16. March 14th was announced as a complete lockdown, but that week, staff went in for two/three days to start/plan remote learning through Google Classroom. During this time, it's been downtime at home since everything besides grocery stores is closed.

During this time, I have been doing remote learning and communicating with students willing to learn through video conferencing. Life is very ironic, and things like your daily life and work are tangible. In January, when Morris said to my face that she didn't want to give me tenure or an extension and she felt my students did not do anything in my classes, I was hurt, and everything was in jeopardy.

The possibility of not having a job in September. From January, it was this anger, sadness, and working my butt off for the extension. However, I dreaded going into that school every morning and feeling the place was hostile because Morris wouldn't say Good Morning to me when I walked into the main office and said GM. It's ironic that now everyone posts Good Morning on the staff's Google Classroom. I would've taken Mata to Gurdwara after school every day since January and prayed for strength, guidance, and a way to resolve this situation. Either grant the extension or find a new workplace or option in September. I needed Babaji to help me because I didn't know what to do. I was lost and didn't know how to help myself with these emotions of thinking she wanted me out, and I sometimes cried in the car driving to Gurdwara on the highway.

However, there was this bigger thing brewing. The COVID-19 virus was spreading, and my first visit was with that kid, Deven, whose mother said she had a relative who came from China to visit who was quarantined. Deven was in and out sick. Another element is going on while I am trying to do my job and fighting for this extension by working hard and carrying my tote bag up and down the stairs. Then comes the unclarity in the mix, the games, and non-optimism through the Union guy (Fekete), so why don't you just try for an open market? She won't give you the extension. He doesn't know I tried open market two years in a row.

Then, the second time, he said I am trying to get you an extension. On the third time, he said, "Make sure this observation is good so I can get you the extension, but look in April and leave if you find something." He said, "She doesn't want to hear you didn't get proper training." On the 4th time, he said she seemed open to the extension after the February break, but it's not due to her observing me before the break. On the 5th time, he said he was informed of my meeting with her and had good and bad news. The Good news was she is giving me the extension. The bad news was she was going to continue the bad observations. He said he told her that if she told her to leave, everyone would know in September; it doesn't look good; it's biased. Immediately, I thought of race and brought up that Brooke and I were doing the speaking field test when Brown gave up and wasn't. Lastly, the next day, I had my meeting with Morris. She was calmer, smiling more, which was different since this virus situation was in the air. Parent-teacher conferences were a question.

I brought up the extension, and she said yes. I told her I signed up for PDs and would start my second Masters. She said it's great I am putting myself out there.

We discussed what she felt was missing from my lesson: a close tie-up. Then, I said you were looking "for closure."

It was an ironic choice of words on my part, and I think she understood and knew it, too. Next week was when schools were declared closed. A state of emergency happened.

When I think of it, the keyword is closure. All my observations were done, and since schools are closed until June, it was a tie-up.

Everything was tied up, and the part I did and the rest of the world, Babaji. She was looking for the type of close and tie-up in my teaching. I guess that is where I think differently. I am a person of Faith and leave things that will all work out. She was a person who did not want to leave anything to work out on her own. There are some things you can't control and need to have Faith. Even though I worked my butt off for that extension by lesson planning until midnight. I also turned to Babaji to pray for things to work out and be okay. The union person said you must play the game, and the other teachers, too. I don't know how to play a game. If you play games with people and confuse them, look, the universe has a bigger game. Please think of this pandemic: we aren't in control; there is something bigger than us always in control. But I still could retain my license. She told me there was the possibility of not returning in September and that I wouldn't have a position, but you still could retain my license. Look what happened now. Who knows what will happen in September with the world? What will September and back-to-school look like if the COVID cases don't go down?

Another element during this time was surfing dating apps and coming across this guy. His pictures looked good, and he looked good. Then it happened, and I got hooked. I went to his Instagram, which was in his profile. I saw all of his pics and saw his name is Daniel Katz. I found him on Facebook; he is a doctor and 26/27 years old. Then, I became the stalker and obsessed as I was with Axel, Manav, Jas's daughter's brother-in-law Gavin.

The strong emotions come when I am doing charts and compatible charts. I googled all the info, and something happened like he changed his Instagram to private. Then, I think he saw that someone he isn't friends with on IG was looking at his stories, so he made it private. I know it's crazy to think that, and I'm making it personal and taking it personally, then I get bummed out, and I think he already has a girlfriend. I called the psychic about Jas's daughter's brother-in-law, and then I found out he had a girlfriend. Now, I don't know how to find out about this fellow. The only reason it's with Jas's daughter's brother-in-law is because of time, and I cried over it already.

Also, this person has now come onto the radar. Then, Babaji, I ask, "Do I do this to myself, or does Babaji bring these people to my radar." The psychic said, "You should feel lucky to see the full picture and how it lays out with those previous people." But what of this person now? Daniel, who I liked on a dating app, can like me back, or is this just a repeat of the previous one? Babaji, you know.

04/14/20

Tuesday

Twenty-five thousand people died in the U.S. today altogether due to COVID-19, continuing this remote learning from home, and it is so abrupt how we left the JHS 167 building without the usual clean up and pack up to end the school year. The ELL office closet I used was just left as is. The supplies and printer I obsessed over and prized over as mine, I left all that as is. I didn't even pack it up. It doesn't really mean or matter. Those things aren't important. The things we get immersed in are so tangible. Even though the 601 students are the ones that teachers dread since their ELLS. Children and kids are who they are.

They are imperfect and can be rude, but we shouldn't categorize or label them. It sucks for the 601 kids and all the kids for their school year to continue like this or to end this way. So abrupt changes are not good for kids. I think of my upbringing and when things like cable or electricity would be out abruptly. It affects you and traumatizes you. I should try to make it better for them. Yet, these ELLS have had rough ordeals and are strong with thick skin.

Also, he leads me to think of Daniel Katz, the person I am now obsessed with. Babaji, am I pathetic to wish and want him? Am I not in reality? Am I being stupid? Someone 9 years younger and I haven't met but just saw on a dating app, FB, and IG, what is wrong

9

with me? Why would I think of someone like they would want me? Since I am the one who grew up with abrupt changes and some effects of trauma. But why can't I, Babaji?

04/15/20

The masks are now mandated and encouraged by Governor Co. Today, remote learning felt like being in the building, and the work was more exhausting than if I were there. This is without getting dressed and driving to work. After talking to students, parents, and teachers/admin, I was still tired. Then, I need to get away, and I think of Daniel. Yes, I go to his social media like he is a celebrity. Then, I was watching Little House on the Prairie and the Albert on Morphine episodes. I have tuned into that show a thousand times in all phases of my life, from the age of 15 till now. I recently wrote this whole script of Albert and Sylvia's storyline and how I wanted it to end. I read it on my laptop, and it was perfect. I couldn't believe I wrote something so real to the characters and got the emotions.

I know that is where I am truly in my element and zone. With this pandemic, this time was an opportunity to focus on myself and my other loves. The opportunity to not get drowned in work and the whole institution. To have the distance of not being engulfed and have boundaries. Today, I felt I was engulfed and was so tired. It felt like being in the building and dealing with everything. I would rather be engulfed in something else. I find things I want, like Daniel and my writing inspirations. When I get engulfed in that, I miss something for work, like I didn't do this or wasn't prepared or organized. I needed to find a way to walk away, and that was this second master's degree, writing, and Daniel. Yet, are these tangible or intangible? Babaji, you know.

The stay-home and quarantine continue during the COVID-19 pandemic. People are dying, and today, I heard of Jaspreet's daughter's brother-in-law passing away, Gavin's brother, who, two months ago, mentioned in this notebook. I mentioned him because I found out Sonam was having a baby two months ago. I started to cry due to everything else that was going on. I wasn't getting an extension; I liked this Gavin, and Ma found out he had a girlfriend. I liked Axel, and he got married and is having a child.

But now, to hear this news, I think back to what that psychic Sim went to. The British woman I asked about Gavin said he doesn't seem right and give you what you need. It didn't work out, and he wasn't even available. The tarot card was the upside kind of sword. But she said also I was lucky to see how things play out. I agree that is a common theme I come across. The redemption, redeemed, and the closure. I feel when something bad happens to me, a bad experience, or people who did me wrong. Babaji brings back those people and brings some light to redeem and settle that bad experience. It is the closure; I think back to Margaret and Eliza Lee, who were bullies in N.P.S 56, and we worked at Rite Aid. Not all of it brings back good news. For this instance, Ma and Rav asked if I felt bad that Ravi's wife got cancer after the Manav wedding. It gives me joy and hope that I understand Babaji. You hear me, and there is evidence by the closure. You hear me about this, Daniel.

We are still staying at home during this quarantine and COVID-19 pandemic. Fifty-six thousand people have passed in the U.S.A., and NYC has lost 12,000. It is Monday today, and I am back to remote learning. I had my one-to-one session with Katsoras and put the video camera on for the conference. I was nervous, and she started with how I went above and beyond to reach the 601 kids.

Then she talked about that 601-team meeting (irrelevant) and 701 and Blake breaking down the lesson with the pull-out.

Of course, I felt defensive, like why was she bringing her up and then the comparison? However, this is all irrelevant now; as we were talking, I told Katsoras who knows about September, and it's a road. I feel I was talking poised and intellectually, but I forget what I say when I am nervous and engrossed. She said she got a new puppy at the end, and I congratulated her. I have to decide and make peace with this JHS 167 situation; I have to stop thinking there is this conspiracy theory of bringing me down and kicking me out, especially since we all got kicked out of the building. It takes me back to what Jenny said. I told her, and she said, "You feel she wants you out." Now, we are all out. All I can say is that if they were biased and had this agenda of throwing me under the bus or targeting me to make work difficult, then there is Karma, and I have to let it go. Blake had her reasons to operate how she does, throwing 6, 7, and 8th on me and having me and Brooke do all the field testing. Those are her reasons, unfortunately, to behave that way. It is unfortunate, and if Millar held this grudge against me, emailing Jenny An based on her not wanting to give me an extension. Then, that is her reason, and that is unfortunate.

Suppose Morris was trying to sabotage a healthy and helpful relationship from forming with Katsoras when I went to K and asked for lesson guidance due to the extension being tentative. In that case, I feel I heard K talking to Morris and saying she went to training. K never set anything up with me, probably because her boss told her. Suppose K gave me development to validate Morris's reason for not wanting to give the extension due to not seeing growth. If Morris and Blake are friends, and she supports her and wants to show she is highly effective, therefore should get the tenure.

All these "ifs," if they are ifs, made up in my head or true, are unfortunate. It's their guilt and conscious. I have to move past it and think beyond it. I have to let it go. I won't forget, and I feel when Brooke said maybe Summit Heights Academy would need her full-time next year, she would be happy not to come back at 167. No one forgets how people and a place made them feel. No one forgets when they were blind-sided or attacked biasedly instead of supported. It goes back to what Oprah said, "When you have given all you can and worked as hard, then you have to let go." I worked hard, and even in January, when she said she wasn't comfortable with the extension, I gave it my all with S.S. + ELA + EWL + ENL. I got the extension, and even now, with the outreaches.

I have to let go because I won't play the game or kiss up. I don't know how to play the game; I just know how to do the work. That's why I started the second master's, again looking at the open market and OLAS. September is tentative, and who knows what is going to be the situation with COVID-19. Morris wanted to make my September employment tentative. She did that in January because I left her office feeling like where I would be in September.

I might not have a job in JHS 167. Look what happened; the world made September tentative. Morris said the rug was pulled under everyone. Well, she pulled the rug under me in January because if I don't get the extension, I can't come back in September or work in District 25, which the union person did not mention. Yet it's their guilt and conscious. It's on them and not on me because I did the work fair.

05/05/20

The pandemic lockdown/ social distancing continues. Schools are still closed until September. We are done for the academic year as I talk to my students every day and worry about them and their concerns. I think about my life, and this (relax/down) time is a reflection or time to reflect on my life. It does feel like those college or school summer days. But I am not 19 or, gosh, even in my twenties. I don't want to talk nonsense. I got tipsy drinking a margarita at home from Kpacho.

13

I thought of Daniel Babaji. I want Daniel, and I know I sound insane. Someone I haven't even met but saw on a dating app and then his social media (IG and FB Someone who is a professional, highly educated, and working hard to be a doctor. Living in the city and experiencing something different. What's wrong with imagining a change/challenge, Babaji?

I need your help, Babaji, because I am close to just sending Daniel a message, "Hey, I saw you on a dating app." Should I do that, Babaji? I fear I might look like a psycho, stalker, or a fool. Should I request him on IG to follow him? Please give me a sign, Babaji!

05/11/20

Still, remote learning will be for the rest of the school year. Babaji, I did not send a request to Daniel. Still waiting for the sign. These two months of working from home have made me do much thinking. Many thoughts like how I was. I do need to work on boundaries. I made LHS167 work, especially because the people there too were personal with LHS167; I do not know if Daniel is a distraction. I just wanted someone I showed interest in to show interest back, regardless of race, creed, or age. I sound like MLK, who is a visionary. Maybe I am visionary in how I see things; it is how I want to see it and not as it is. It could very much be that Daniel is just busy with his residency and did not see my "Like."

Babaji, we both know that I will continue to think of him. Babaji, I do not know why I do this, but I do it to myself. Maybe this is my realization that I am ready to date, but I just want to date Daniel. I did the charts, tarot, and astrology.

14

The emotions were a bit more real yesterday (05/12/2023). In the morning, I was watching the De Blasio conference and picked some Indian doctors to run a tracing program. Then I looked him up, and he did a residency in Presbyterian. He met his wife there, who is white. Then, I got emotional as I walked around my room and looked at Babaji's picture. Asking how I got here and thinking of Daniel. He can meet someone in residency, so why would he be interested in me? Then, I started regretting and thinking of the past. I think of when I was 25 and what did I do wrong that I am here. What I wanted and where I was. Daniel brings such an emotion and fixation right now. Even a video conference meeting with the other 601 screaming teachers did not flinch me too much because I was far ---- to escape. Working from home has protected me from the drama-filled environment at 167, for which I take some responsibility.

Then, something happened in the evening or close to the evening. Daniel's Instagram became public. I was so happy that I went downstairs and concealed my joy as Rav followed Jordan and crawled all over the kitchen and the house. I was so excited to go upstairs like I would see my crush or he came back. I saw the rest of his pics, and it was a strong, nervous emotion as I was laying in my bed and thinking of him. Babaji, it was a sign that I should follow him, and I did with an alternative IG account that is public, which I did not know and had no posts/followers. Babaji, what is happening here? Is it that I can still revert to the behavior of a schoolgirl? I am just daydreaming of us being together with such strong emotions for Daniel.

In addition, I don't even think there is something wrong with that. Babaji, I am looking for signs, and everything is becoming one. Yesterday's episode of Little House of Eliza Jane loving a man who did not love her. Babaji, am I Eliza Jane here? Delusional? In a snap reality, Rav is talking to me about Sim's deal. She has been here for

15

a year and does not pay for anything. The same song but with different lyrics. Papa complains about his health, and Ma yells at him. I realize the dysfunction that I pushed to forget by thinking of Daniel.

However, I can do something about it now. I do not have to get involved in the conversation with Rav that is so familiar. Babaji, am I wrong? To see Daniel and want more? Want out, which is not ideal. I have to find my way out. Babaji, I was painting a new picture with Daniel, and I am not wrong. Babaji, what do you want for me? Stay here or move? When I checked D's Instagram this morning, it went to private. Maybe he saw my alternative account following or unfollowing. Babaji, I still wish and dream. Maybe it is childish that I still have that ability to escape. What life do you want for me, Babaji? There with my folks and Rav, Sim, Cole, and Jordan, or move? Babaji, was I foolish to even paint a picture with Daniel? I have tried not to be an extension of anyone in my family. To put it in perspective, those are their lives or choices. I don't reflect or am them.

05/14/20

Babaji, I think of Daniel starting in the afternoon to now evening. The emotions/feelings are so strong; I do not think I can slip away from this because I want this. Please, Babaji, help me find a way for him or me.

Destiny and Faith are to be tested now, Babaji. The most miraculous thing would be that I injured my knee and went to Presbyterian, and Daniel is there. We meet, and that is where it starts. That would be something. I do not think I can let this go, Babaji. Give me a sign, but not just that, let this be, Babaji. Let this be!

If this is not to be, why Babaji did Daniel appear in front of me on a dating app? If he did not pop on my screen phone, but he did. Babaji, it would not be fair. It just would not be fair.

I told Rav and Sim about Daniel Katz. Sim said why did you like the person and then delete your account? She said that I should be confident. I told them it was because of the age difference. Rav said it does not matter and that online dating can be fun. It made me feel better, telling them instead of keeping all these emotions for this fellow inside. It gives me hope for Daniel or, with regard to him, Babaji. Especially since it was after the British Psychic said he was emotionally immature and brought up the age gap. Note to self: Do not ever go to the British Psychic again. I really am trying to let go of this past baggage and listen to my calling and follow my calling or the mothership, which is my soul, Babaji. I think of UNICEF education for girls and other callings like writing, storytelling, and films.

05/17/20

Babaji, I am starting to lose hope for Daniel Katz. Babaji, I just wanted a chance with him, to meet him and talk with him. I just wanted to like someone and him to like me back. I can't let this/him go, Babaji. What am I to do? What if I can't find it on Dating apps again? I went to Manhattan with Jordan today so he could visit his father. While sitting in the car, I noticed the quiet, empty streets, a result of the COVID-19 pandemic.

I thought, am I not to have that – *city life with a beau* (American)? Is perhaps not possible due to what? I grew up with straight dysfunction or non-normalcy. When did I get into the city and American Beau? Babaji, I need your help; please, bring me Daniel. Please give me a sign.

Babaji and God, I am still waiting for a sign of if I should request Daniel on Instagram or Facebook. Please give me an indication, Babaji and God. Here, I am doing my remote learning, and on the side, I am searching for Daniel's profile on Various dating apps again. Searching through all these profiles for his, I am thinking, why didn't I screenshot his profile when I first saw it or read it more thoroughly? I got so excited. I have felt so hard for Daniel. Someone who I haven't talked to or met in person. Babaji and God let Daniel come and be. Let my craziness be, or this be. I don't want to let Daniel go. I just got so invested and obsessed with him that I feel it's right, and I know him already. Please, Babaji and God, I don't want to get hurt or be let down.

Babaji and God, I requested to follow Daniel on Instagram yesterday. It was evening, and I was thinking about "closure" and "putting myself out there." Words from that meeting with Morris when she gave me the extension. Those were the words I took away from that. How powerful those words are that they just aligned to now. She said, "It's good that you are putting yourself out there." I felt I needed to take the step and see what happens so I can know. If he did not accept, then I can have closure/peace.

After I requested, I prayed not to get hurt. Let this go my way. Let the visions and reality align Babaji and God. Then, I got the notification tonight that he accepted my request.

While Rav, Sim, and I are telling Papa that metformin is causing him to lose weight. The noise, but I know I am going extreme or ahead here. I took mata in the afternoon for myself, Ros, Sim, Cole, Jordan, and Ma, for all our health, peace, and happiness. I just wanted to change the way I do things. Regarding Axel and Manav, I couldn't express what I wanted and didn't put myself out there or take the first step. So, I became a stalker and checked their social media. When they got with others, I got upset over nothing between us because there was no interaction/contact. I got upset because I couldn't or didn't express or put myself out there. I imagined without doing anything, and I want to be in reality and want things to be real. When I got the notification, Babaji, I was happy myself.

05/24/20

The NY Times cover was sad today, with three pages dedicated to 1,000 names (1%) of the lives passed due to COVID-19 virus. The headline had the word "incalculable?" Many things in life are incalculable, enormous, immense, and untold. The situation Papa has created is immense but understandable. He lost weight and is anxious. However, I want to think about myself and not about Papa and my parents. I want to be selfish this time around. Babaji and God, yesterday, when Daniel accepted my request, it brought all these emotions. Now, I wouldn't say I liked a pic of his since Rav said to only like current ones that show up on the stream. Daniel hasn't requested to follow me on IG. Now, what lies beneath him accepting my request is to be known. If it is a genuine likeness on his post or if he accepts all chick's requests. So he can have a lot of followers is unknown. I have to focus on this now, and I want to Babaji and God. I want Daniel, and I don't want to jump ahead, and there is fear, but there is also positivity and belief, Babaji and God.

Babaji and God, I am going to be patient and work on myself to be the best version of myself and give the best expression. Daniel accepted my request. Now, how can I have him follow me and message me? I leave that somewhat to you, Babaji, and God. I know you will provide me with the way and be the power behind it so that I have the opportunity and chance to talk to Daniel. I will continue to stay positive, believe, and have faith in Daniel as the opportunity and chance that will come to me, just as many things will come to me, Babaji, and God.

I will be patient, Babaji and God. I sent a "Hi" to Daniel on Instagram yesterday. All the emotions and waiting that led me to put myself out there resulted in me messaging "Hi." I haven't heard anything back yet. I am going to continue to believe and be patient, Babaji and God. Daniel will come when I am my best version and confident. I feel I am already slightly there. This is what I want, Babaji and God. I believe in and am listening to my intuition, that's why I messaged him, so I don't fear because I believe. I am not scared. The day before yesterday, 10000 people in total died from COVID-19 in the USA. Today, due to an African American dying by the police led to protests and fires. So much is going on in the world. Amidst it all, I think of this and want this: Daniel, chance, opportunity, Babaji, and God.

Violent protests today are so scary and sad… what is happening in this country along with COVID-19? It pisses me off to see the looting when we as a country have been sitting home since March of social distancing, only to allow protests and looting. COVID-19 is over, then open NYC tomorrow. Before this evening's news, I thought of Daniel; I felt that since last Saturday, when he accepted my IG request, today (Saturday), he would reply to my "Hi."

I got angry and dismantled myself. Not skinny, not pretty, not white. However, I am beautiful, and everything is awesome for Daniel. I am just not his level, but higher than that. I am beautiful, with great hair and an intelligent mind. So, I surrender to you, Babaji, and God of all, about Daniel. I liked it, requested it, and said "Hi" to Daniel—all those things to Daniel and more, Babaji and God. Now, I surrender Babaji, and God, I surrender.

Babaji and God, first let Papa gain weight, get his energy back, and be healthy. Second, let there be peace in the city and around this country from violent protests. I have been trying hard to be positive and not throw the towel since March 15th, when the world shut down. Not going to the 167 building and working from home has, in a way, been this time to reflect internally and externally. These two and half months have been of gratitude. First, I am truly grateful to have been allowed to reflect by being distant from the distraction of 167. It brought me to my school days of how I was and all I wanted.

All those things to Daniel and more Babaji and God. Now, I surrender to Babaji and God. I surrender.

Coming across Daniel during this time made me realize what I want now. The things I want now, Babaji and God, are an extension of things I wanted that were buried inside and now have come out. I buried them, Babaji and God. I allowed work, 167, and any other distraction/nonsense (Sonam shower, Axel &, etc.) to be on the surface. Now that I and we all are distant from that, what I wanted, which was buried, has surfaced. Now, these are the things I want, and I feel when things go back to normal, I can't go back to the way I was and the way I was functioning/living. I would love to meet/talk to Daniel, Babaji and God, mainly because of what I do know about myself now. I know it's my time, and I am positive. It's not too late, and just like teacher Max said, she spent time with her husband during the weekend upstate. That I can say about that kind of love for myself. I believe in Babaji and God. I surrender because I know you don't have me stuck or will have me stuck. I am not stuck and, Babaji/God, you have heard my wish with regard to Daniel. So I surrender, Babaji/God.

6/4/20

COVID and now Black Lives Matter protests & looting, and a curfew of 8 pm. Amongst all this, today was a hard day since it was Clerical Day when we had meetings, so we did them remotely. The staff meeting was about race. Then it got hard; with everything going on in the world, I was intimidated by these people at work. I can't show my face by turning on the camera or talking. Then I get upset that I shut down. Also, I am thinking of Daniel, Babaji, and God. I messaged, I sent the request, and he accepted, and I liked a pic. Now, it's to the universe, Babaji, and God for Daniel to respond. Sim said it sounds like I have a crush. I have a crush at this point in my life. Sim said it was okay. Babaji and God, it is okay because at least I took some action with regard to my emotions and feelings after seeing Daniel. I am not scared or angry, Babaji and God, because I know I can be patient for the things I want to manifest, and now I want to be. I hope for Daniel and will continue to, Babaji and God.

6/9/20

I surrender, and today I thought of requesting Daniel on Facebook, but I can't do that because, God, it would look like stalking, I believe. God and Babaji you need to give me the answers with regards to this and Daniel. I said I would be patient because I want to be the best version of myself when (if) I am to meet Daniel. I need to continue to do the work to be the best version of myself. My authentic and best self. I am to be the best authentic version of myself when meeting Daniel. Otherwise, there would be no point, I believe, Babaji and God. I feel so much, want so much and never put myself out there than I have with Daniel. I feel so much and want this so much, and for the first time, I put myself out there with Daniel by requesting him and messaging him. Babaji and God, Daniel needs to respond, please. Babaji and God, do I need to request him on FB. Babaji and God, show me the way or bring the way to me.

6/11/20

Almost 100 days since shut down due to COVID-19. Last night, I was tossing and turning with just these thoughts and impromptu convos I am having with various people. With myself, the LHS167 staff, and my family. Then, in the dark, I just said out loud, God and Babaji, I feel I am going to marry Daniel Katz, and Babaji and God, my purpose and my calling is to write, tell stories, and tell my stories. Then I thought about this remote learning time and that is a story in itself. I imagined telling Morris that I should get tenure due to the three moments/students that stick out and I will never forget. John, Jing, and Emma. Those three define this remote learning. I was thinking of writing an op-ed about John, not having the Wi-Fi, Emma moving around, and Jing's cracked cell phone while doing assignments. Babaji and God, I want to write this op-ed. Give me the strength to write eloquent words to show how brave those three are, God and Babaji. In a way, I realized how strong/brave I am, and I am a damn good teacher. Now the other happening was this guy who messaged me on a dating app.

Basically said I was beautiful and cute and asked if I wanted FWB. I said no, that is not what I am looking for. Then he said sorry, and I said directly/confidently you should be honest & upfront. He said you seem like a nice person. I was glad that it ended the convo, and I didn't take it personally, and I kept my power. I felt like, ok, Babaji and God, you have still cleared the path for Daniel. I have been thinking about Daniel, Babaji, and God. I still believe. I have hope, and I have my intuition and my faith, Babaji and God.

6/15/20

I was crying all of last night. I got angry and upset. Just so much going through my head. Thoughts of Daniel, and then I am creating moments and scenes with Daniel. One where he went to a party in the city and left to see me because he was thinking of me. That is when it dawned on me that we weren't in normal times. Daniel or anybody can't go to a city party. Nightlife isn't happening right now due to COVID-19 quarantine/social distancing at the moment, that is the clash of him going to a party at a club/lounge and me talking about teaching remote summer school. If there is remote, then there is no nightlife. I realize that I am being selfish. Crying over what I don't have, feeling sorry for myself. I get it from Papa since, during this time, he is fixated on how he isn't feeling well and constantly telling Ma, Rav, and me about his bowel problems and that something is wrong with him.

He stresses us, and it could be very much that this quarantining & staying at home is worsening the social anxiety where Papa doesn't want to step out and do things that are open/possible like grocery shopping, car wash, walks, and long car drives. It's easy to live in your cocoon and just think about yourself and your problems instead of taking in what's going on around/outside with other people. I am lucky to have work/interaction with the 601 students. To hear their stories and to help them. Sim was right; I was lucky and am because even September is not going to be normal. In this morning's meeting, Morris said it's blended learning with 540 people capacity. Here, I am looking for openings, and that's not the solution or even relevant right now if September is remote. I am just trying to fill some void or satisfy this idea that my life sucks or it has problems. I am being selfish, thinking about what's wrong with my life and thinking about things I don't have and want. Getting upset about why Daniel didn't reply/respond to my IG message. This is not a normal time; so much is going on, and so much of what was normal has disappeared. Stores boarded and closed.

Yes, these three months allowed me to deeply feel what is missing and the work I need to do. I was able to reflect on who my authentic self is and what she wants from life. However, the work to get it has to be done when things are normal. It's like that guy who wanted FWB. He was selfish and thinking of his own wants during a time of COVID 19 when people weren't choosing to interact with strangers and were socially distancing for their health and families' health. To those people choosing to protest and loot. To those people on apps trying to meet someone during COVID 10 quarantining. There is a time and place. Perhaps Daniel is not selfish, and he understands time/place, so he didn't respond or even check the message; only God knows, but crying like someone died last night over Daniel not responding to my message is me being selfish when so many people have died due to COVID 19.

It's me thinking about what I want, what will make me happy, and my happiness. This is the time and place to say thank you. Going to gurdwara and praying for a want (Daniel), it should be more towards than you, and I have been lucky. Thank you. I have my job, my salary, helping 601 kids, and the opportunity to hear their stories (John, Emma, and Jing). I need to write that op-ed. Thank you for taking time home/cocoon to reflect and be removed from the normal routine of getting up & going to work. This is the time to look more outward than inward. To be someone of service. Yes, there are elements of my life that I thought of last night that led me to tears. The biggest fear of being stuck, but I can fix that. What is stuck? If that is the fear, then by looking at the universe has been on my side. In those three months of Jan, Feb, & March, I felt stuck in a whole of not feeling like I was a good teacher or good at my job. March came, I got the extension, and COVID-19 removed everyone from their holes. Daniel hasn't replied/responded to my message yet (I am still hopeful!) Daniel accepted my IG request. Someone I haven't spoken to, and if he hadn't, that would have really hurt. To be really

7/18/20

Ode to sisters:

Raveena and Simran, you raised me. Protected me and looked out for me; Simran bought me express clothes in high school so I would look like I dressed well. Who does that? Raveena completed my wants because she wanted to make me happy. Who does that? Raveena was thrown with the financial responsibility of running the household. Making sure that doesn't happen to me. Who does that? So far, from what I have seen and learned. No sister does that. No one does that. Even a year ago, my sisters were telling me that even though they didn't have a wedding, I still could and that I shouldn't think I couldn't either.

They didn't want me to think I couldn't have everything or at least that. They didn't want me to be bitter. Who does that? They could have easily said you too Harleen, since I am the sibling too, and accept some fate or pattern. But they always wanted to give me options. Who does that? My sisters did that. Raveena and Simran, I owe you.

I always prayed to God to give you everything you want and ten times more. Jordan came, and I felt it was just a fraction of my wish

26

to God/Babaji to give Raveena what she wanted and ten times more. When more comes, I will be cheering the loudest. I know there is more. Raveena is so happy, and I feel we are both not emotionally stuck anymore. My sisters didn't want me to be stuck even though they, at most times, felt stuck. Who does that? People are always looking and wondering if they have a guardian angel looking out for them. I, at 7 years old, knew I had two guardian angels looking out for me.

My guardian angels are my sisters. I told Raveena that you are free now and don't have to worry about me anymore. You have Jordan and raise him. Don't have to look out for me anymore. Everything you have taught me and the experiences we have gone through. How you carried yourself and your actions with others. It's all with me and inside me. I take it with me, so don't worry. I owe you, and for a while, that is all I knew. It was the driving force of my actions. The jobs I had and the career I ended up choosing.

I felt I needed to help, too, and I owed it to my sisters and our parents. But Raveena still made me feel reassured that you need to do something for yourself. However, I still carried on with that mantra. I realized I would not be truly happy with that mantra. (I realized what it feels like to be stuck and not feeling fulfilled or completely happy now working as a teacher. I am content and can get by, but I still dream and dream big. There is still that calling for the writing, storytelling and writing scripts. Stories, my stories.)

March

Schools went remote, and I was still angry about the Morris situation. Sitting home and reflecting on my life. Realizing the job was consuming my life. Now, with not going to work, I felt something was missing and thought of my love life. I got scared that what if now I never meet anyone. Realized I needed to be the best version of myself and do that work. Need to change & think about what Zully said about looking towards non-Indians. Thought about my response. Thought about needing to put myself out there. Saw Daniel and swiped like. Thought how Daniel is non-Indian, unlike Axel, Manav, & Gavin. Went deep into spirituality and the soul. Read & watched Gavin Zukov & Oprah. Got scared of rejection and my inexperienced dating past, so I deleted the profile and told Rav & Sim about Daniel. Sim said to be confident, and Rav said it would be okay. Created a new profile. Turned to God & Babaji and said I don't know, but I know you know. Requested Daniel on IG. Papa was talking about his health and not feeling good in the evening with Rav & Sim. I was in the room when I got the notification that he accepted. I was giddy, and the energy helped me continue working on myself and losing weight. I messaged Daniel, "Hi," and not wanting to consume myself.

May

I was just proud that I put myself out there, and so far, I was happy with the cause & effect. The outcome went in my favor, and he accepted. I can't complain. Ma told me about some Arizona guy & I said I didn't want a Sardar. Ma and I talked, and I told her I wanted to find someone/meet on my own. Ma said yes, with what she sees going on around her circle, everyone should and Ma said she will accept whoever and she will support me.

June

I chatted with other guys online, and all were positive. Said how beautiful I am and how young I look (25-27, one guy said). I spoke to one on the phone. Told Rav that I don't want to settle for someone who doesn't have the things I want (stability). Rav said this is a good start that I am talking on the phone.

July

I expressed my fear of what if there weren't others, and Rav said there would be. Had dreams where, in one, Daniel had his hands up in surrender. Another dream of two Jewish men talking to me in suits.

Things I realized:

- When I was 13, I would tell Ma & Shreya that I didn't need to date, that I believed in soulmates, and God would bring the person.
- When you realize what you want, it is liberating and an awakening.
- The universe & God is waiting for you to live, to change your best (version) meant for you. Mo made fun by saying if you get into a car accident is that person who is meant for you, and I said yes.
- The reason my love life is obsolete or empty is because I was not the best version of myself. I spent time being angry with situations and circumstances that were presented to me. I wasn't courageous. That is why I decided to leave it to Ma, and she would take care of it (arranged)
- Axel, Manav & Gavin, and even people MA told me about & the one I met for dinner didn't work out because those didn't match/fit my authentic self that I didn't realize when I thought they were it.

- Surrender, believe, and apologize to God for not accepting and welcoming what God flowed my way.
- You can come to your conclusions & assumptions, things, but God will want more.
- God prepares you by presenting the situations and circumstances you will be in.
- Apologize to God for being angry about the circumstances & situations that were brought instead of understanding that this is what God wants for me now. There is a reason.
- Restore the faith in God that I will welcome & embrace what you bring because that is what you want me to understand so I can understand my authentic self better.
- Apologize that I didn't have gratitude, appreciate the things God brought to me, and invest my 100%.
- People will write you off and question how you got certain things in your life, but I shouldn't do the same.
- Apologize to God for questioning how I got this. (LHS167 job). Questioning the good things, when I should embrace, say I deserve it & deserve to be here.
- I am courageous for putting myself out there.

This morning, I felt good, and Papa got his stress test, and his heart is fine. I felt positive and not too consumed with Daniel. It was a positive consumption where I reflected on all the things I wrote on the previous page. God & Babaji, was I courageous enough to request Daniel & send him a message? Or was that a sign of how I was when I wrote those messages to (Sonam & Ravi & Nisha). I feel shame writing their names. I can't compare the two. Go, I know you don't want me to feel that way, shamed, scared that I can't have love or a relationship or a future. I know you do, God, and I know you have forgiven me for doing those things. God, I ask, are those dreams signs? Doubt is coming, but I am still holding on and hoping for Daniel because I followed my intuition.

I remember being 12 years old and walking home from school. (Every day) during a normal week, I would come home to something being cut, either the cable or electricity. I made it a game and titled it "What will be cut off today?" this could be the first line of my book or screenplay.

Now, how do I even start describing today? I woke up this morning, and Rav took off to take Papa to the doctor. Papa started with the usual antics. I just felt bad and angry because I knew Rav didn't want to leave Jordan. So, I yelled at Papa and said, "Die." I regret it, God and Babaji, but I got so angry. I, like usual, felt I needed to protect Rav and fight her fights. This has just been on going of how Papa hasn't changed, and it's the same things/pattern/life.

Later in the afternoon, Rav, Cole, Jordan, and I went to have lunch. I had two margaritas, and in the car, I was just looking at Daniel's IG pics. I just kept thinking and wishing how I wanted him to respond to my message & reach out to me.

Then we got home, and Papa was sitting in the room. I just went to the IG of this girl who he went to dinner with and who his cousin tagged. Then there was a pic of her and Daniel in a kiss. She wrote along the lines of moving to a new city, a new job and meeting him. Daniel had a comment: "Love you." Then I went to Daniel's IG, and he had nothing, not even a pic of her. my tears started, and seeing Papa in front of me, I went upstairs to my room. I took Babaji's picture off the wall and said, "I don't believe in God or Babaji anymore." I laid the picture on the bed in Jordan's room. I sat on the rocking chair and cried like a baby, like someone stabbed me or died. I am looking at Babaji's picture and asking, "Why? I don't get it." How can my intuition be wrong? I have been hoping and praying to Babaji and God that Daniel will reach out to me. I spent energy, prayers, and money on charts & psychics, tarots, thoughts on images, thinking of him and our future, and that Daniel Katz would reach out to me. Then I am saying to Babaji and God that I am stupid that I created something and didn't see things as they are. If Daniel wanted to reach out then he would have replied to my message. But yet, I was hoping and praying that he would. I don't get it, Babaji, and God, I thought you wanted this for me.

I put myself out there. I felt messaging Daniel was courageous of me. So then, why this, Babaji and God? I deleted all my dating apps from my phone. I thought about Manjot, Manav, and Gavin. Starting to feel even more stupid by putting this in that category. When I got downstairs, I felt empty and hurt. It really hurts, Babaji and God. I kept looking at Guru Nanak's picture and thinking of Daniel crying. Ras picked up on my low spirit and saw me crying. She instantly brought up the doctor, and I told her everything. She said you can't put this in the same category as those three because you actually talked to someone on the phone. She said not to delete the apps and keep looking.

Babaji and God, I don't want to look. Babaji and God, I want Daniel. I can't believe and accept that my intuition was wrong. The day I saw him, I became so positive and awakened to my authentic self, soul, spirit, and my calling. I wanted to do the work to be my best version and started. I don't get it, Babaji and God. What about those dreams? Daniel surrendered with his hands up and the two Jewish men. I don't understand, Babaji and God. I thank Daniel for awakening me by just looking at his pic, but I can't believe that is the only purpose for Daniel. I can't believe that's it. My intuition says differently. I don't know what's to be with Daniel and this chick. Perhaps I can be happy for people finding love. My intuition says not to forget Daniel. Babaji and God, I can be patient, and I will still hope for Daniel and me.

Riverhead Vineyard with Jordan

Oh Papa, Papa, Papa has become something due to not feeling well and losing weight. Papa doesn't want to go anywhere. I thik the source of this has been the source this whole time. Papa doesn't know how to solve problems. Problems come and then he becomes negative/angry/bitter and looks to others to solve them. It was the case with the financial problems, but no one could fix his health. He needs to do that. I try to do what I can for Papa, but I can't invest completely. I need to focus on my life, and so much time was invested focusing on our parents and their issues/problems. We couldn't focus on our lives. However, I can't help but se the things he does and be reminded of the times I did those things. Papa called constantly to tell us to drive back home on our way to the vineyard. Babaji, I did that when I would text Ma constantly about coming back from this person's reception/party.

Papa is depressed and does not want to go anywhere. Babaji, I did that, but the only difference is that I did it when it was somewhat appropriate. In my twenties, when I was going through stuff. Papa is behaving this way in his seventies. Babaji, it makes me realize how much I hurt Mami, and I am sorry for that, Babaji. It scares me, Babaji, is that in me: giving up, becoming biter/negative, regretting, and falling from grace. However, I can't say that, Babaji, because I didn't give up earlier this year when the tenure/extension situation occurred. I can say right now, and these past few months I have been the most positive.

Last night, I got this intense positive feeling, Babaji, that I shouldn't give up on Daniel. Even though the real artifacts are there of that picture with the girl, I still have hope, and my mind can be devoted to all the images I can create all day where I am narrating our story or (vows) with the most mature, profound, and eloquent words.

33

However, the images are images, and what I seek is for them to be real. The real world feels better, and I am not asking for all the images, but to experience it for real would be nice, Babaji. I can create what I can create. I can do what I can to make them real/reality, but you can help, Babaji, by putting a hand to make it a real experience I can live. That's all I want is to live. I will continue to hope and have blind faith.

8/9/20

I took away two things: this intense positive energy and intelligence. Suddenly, all the things I wanted became activated and urgent. To be the best version of myself became necessary. I can't explain the effect, and I sought/wanted some clarity on how you were different from the others I was drawn to. It really is due to that I didn't know what I wanted then. I wasn't aware of who I was and my authentic self. Your simple comments and statements reminded me of what I believed when I was younger and how I felt my stories could help someone not feel alone in a similar situation or circumstances. Your being made me feel like how I was as a child or just younger. When you are 12 and talking to con ed for the electricity to come on makes it difficult to think about someone, sowhere is made for you. It's hard to think about fantasy or fantasize when you are dealing with reality. Babaji and God, I wrote some of those eloquent words I imagine saying to Daniel. I am proud and not ashamed. Even though I don't have a realistic artifact to validate how I feel. I am having my heart and intuition validate. There is nothing in reality or realistic in my favor, Babaji and God, but just my hope and faith.

It was necessary for me to be positive. Through your energy I felt all those beliefs I had when I was younger that felt weren't relevant anymore. I realized they were more than ever relevant and valid because they made me positive and represented my authentic self. When we connect, all other relations are doomed because no one can stand in the way of energy.

11:38 pm

Babaji, I was lying on the bed in the dark. I was watching YouTube videos of tarot readings in August for Libra and Sag separately. I was about to put my phone down, but I checked my Instagram and saw Daniel had a story. I looked, and it was him in scrubs with the caption after 13-hour surgery. Then I thought maybe I should reply with appropriate applause emoji. But then I stopped and closed my phone, and then I asked Babaji if I should send an emoji & said, "ini mini miny mo." Then I just did it & sent the applause emoji. Then I was like, maybe I should unsend it, but then I saw the notification; Daniel reacted to the emoji with a heart.

I got out of bed, turned the light on, and put my head to Babaji's picture and said, "Thank you, Babaji," over and over. I got a response or something, Babaji. I said, Babaji, you are going to help me with this. Babaji, you are going to guide my steps & not have me do anything wrong. I was so giddy and jumping up and down in front of Babaji's picture. I was still on this high that I was pacing the room, just saying, "What am I going to do?" and "I can't believe it." My emotions are in check now, Babaji. Thank you, but there is still that other picture. Babaji is Daniel, genuine & kind, or a player. I don't know, but Babaji and God, you do. Thank you for giving me this moment and experience of giddy like a school girl, I think, and joy, Babaji and God. I wouldn't describe it school girl, though. It's cause and effect. It's giving and receiving. It's wishing and getting your want and wish. Thank you for this moment.

After yesterday's moment at night, I had a dream. Daniel was sending messages and asking me out. Babaji and God, another dream. Babaji and God, I am tired now from all the imaging, watching tarot videos, and all the psychics. Babaji and God, can you now just please let what needs to happen happen. I need to rest now, and I need my focus back. I didn't pass the test again for WGU. So, Babaji and God, can you just let what is to happen for real happen. I thank you, Babaji and God, for saving me today from being bound.

Rav gave my info to the mortgage guy for buying a house. But it didn't go through since my credit balances are high. Rav has to buy the house under only her info. Babaji and God, I feel that as the ultimate sign from you it is my time to move forward with my life just like I expressed to Rav. Afterward, Rav said the same to Mami: how long is Harleen going to stay with us? She is going to move on, too. Babaji and God, I do feel that I feel the spirit and understand that this is my time to move on with regards to being in a relationship and partnership (bound). I didn't feel it in the first three months of this year because I was dealing with a toxic work situation. It came to me in March after I saw Daniel's picture and profile. There are clues and signs everywhere. Kerri said to Rav on the phone that you shouldn't put on the mortgage because what if in the 1-3 years she gets married, then it will be hard to take me out. Signs are also feelings that the universe is giving me. Babaji and God, now I am just exhausted mentally with all the energy I have used. I am ready for what is to happen to happen.

Yesterday, when I went to Central Park Zoo, I was anxious/nervous. Babaji and God, I think it had to do with knowing Daniel is in Manhattan. Then I let my mind wander. What if I see him? Then, walking to Central Park to see on one side (right) Sih protestors for Khalistan and, on my left, a group of people coming out of the temple. What was that, Babaji? Today, the weather was very fallish, and it reminds me that summer is almost over. Schools are going to open, and I welcome work to keep me busy. Babaji and God, I feel I am more balanced now, and the reality of where & what my life consists of now is with me. Yes, I have my hopes for what I want in my life when Sept comes and even now. Even though I didn't do "ini mini" today, the hope, daydreaming & dreams still live. The belief is still there. Babaji and God, the heart emoji that Daniel sent, gave me something real vs. something I imagined or created.

I am grateful for that because it stopped the "ini mini." Now I feel it's his turn since I requested him, and I sent the emoji. If he wants further then he needs to reach out. Babaji, I think that is what's fair and right. I can't just be doing the pursuing, and it has to be a two-way street. Babaji, these past five months of the pandemic allowed me to really heal and be the best version of myself by losing weight and growing spiritually, mentally, and emotionally (physically). Thinking of the past but making peace with it by wanting/declaring that I want to move forward with my life. I want my life to move forward. Seeing Daniel and pouring all these emotions and energy awakened me to imagine the life I want and the things I want. Now, social media/apps starting something genuine/real is what I leave you to answer, Babaji, but I feel these five months served a purpose.

Clarity

Babaji and God, I really just want to talk about myself here. Today I finished the Raod Home screenplay and emailed the prof. He wrote that he was very proud that I finished and to keep it up (writing). I am proud that I finished it and want to submit it to contests. Haven't been doing the 'ini-mini' and, according to Rav, the obsessing. Been focusing on the WGU and this screenplay. Rav's convo the other night provided clarity. We talked about Papa and focusing on them most of our lives. Rav asked if my obsessing was an escape mechanism because she was going out constantly. We talked about Axel & Manav. I told her how, after college, I wanted to go away to film school. I knew that I didn't want to follow like her friend's kids. But it didn't work out for me then, and I stayed & went to St. John's. With Axel, it was because I saw people my age getting married, and I thought I was to do that. I got stuck in Mom's world and thought I was an extension of her. In my thoughts, I didn't imagine a future with Axel.

Then, when Saachi married him, I thought it was a missed opportunity. Even though Ma asked me and I rejected/refused. Then, Manav, I thought it was a redemption, but I didn't imagine a future. I didn't know who I was, my identity, or what I authentically wanted. I felt I was an extension of Mom. Then, with Jas's daughter's bro-law, it was again looking at the wrong things. Babaji and God, I am glad you gave me the time & journey to find my authentic self. I told Rav the messages I wrote were more what Ma and my relationship. I was angry at her. I felt she didn't have my back or my side. I felt like an extension of her, and I blamed her & was angry at her. The best way I can put it is I didn't want to be like her, but I felt no choice, and instead of changing my choice, I wanted her to change. Recently, Ma somehow did. During this pandemic, for Ma to tell me how the mom of that huy in India liked my FB picture.

I told her I should remove her, and Rav said no. Ma started talking about that guy and the family. I told Ma that I wanted to find someone on my own, and I felt I could. Ma said you should, everyone should, and that is how it should be. Her society came up, and Ma said what's going on there is a mess. I told Rav that I was proud of myself and that despite Papa's negative attitude, I didn't succumb like I would have in the past. I stayed positive, lost myself a bit with the obsessive thinking, and brought some pain and heartache. Babaji and God, I was hoping, and I feel even the creating/imagining reflected my authentic self. I feel there was genuine behind it. The desire to ant and feel a connection of some sort.

I felt on Saturday when I was crossing the street with Jordan, Rav, & Dogi on the right, and the guy on the Citi bike with neon sunglasses was Daniel. Babaji and God, I feel it was. Truly, only you know, Babaji and God. Yes, I want someone/something & this is something too. They all boost comfort and not ego.

In the fall, going to work or going remote, I am going with something, and that is the transformative self that I worked on. I don't agree with Rav that I have an ego to chase an image. I do have an ego to be affected, awakened by people to be a better version of myself. To be inspired and to learn. I was also reminded of things I see at work. Middle school girls have so many issues because of the toxic problems at home. Girls who carry it with them throughout life. I am lucky; even though our parents had financial issues, I had a support system that didn't allow me to carry it, and I was able to focus on my education and not be taken advantage of or labeled. I was allowed & able to be something.

Yesterday, teachers had to report to school/work without students. Seeing the changes in the building with hand sanitizer dispensers & 6ft social distancing mats on the floor. Seeing the familiar faces since it will be 4 years at 167 on Nov. 7th. Babaji & God, I understand why starting at a new school wouldn't have been wise. It's nice to see faces that have become familiar and known during a school year like this. Even though there was nothing to do, I used the time and was able to focus & make flashcards for the WGU test. At home, there is too much to do & the (distraction) of Papa's depression. Going to work allows me to focus. Babaji & God, that is why I feel this home is not allowing me to serve my purpose. I am good on my own and removed even though I have a garment on from my liposuction on Friday.

I need work to focus. Rav said that the obsession with Daniel was due to escaping from the stuff going on at home. I don't feel that is true. Babaji & God, I was thinking of Daniel in the school library today. Thinking of him makes me feel this energy, and I am confident. I know it's also the work I have done on myself. The investing and realizing I need to embrace what I have & where I am. I deserve to be at 167 and need to give my 100% to what God/Babaji has sent my way. I sent Daniel a wave emoji, but he didn't react. Babaji and God, I don't feel any different about Daniel. I just put myself out there. I don't feel lost or like a fool. I don't feel this is the end, Babaji and God. When my mind was clear and calm which it was after spending the day with two senior teachers in the library (Jules & Rosenberg), I still felt hope and love for myself. Babaji and God, that is even bigger & better.

Papa was throwing up at home. Rav and Ma said that the ambulance should be called so Papa could go to the hospital. Rav told me to take Cole for a walk since he needed to go for one. So I took him and I remember getting to the next block and being able to see the ambulance come to the house. Cole was sniffing a bush, and the ambulance went past me down the road. I think I mouthed "Papa" since I knew he was in the ambulance. Then I said, "Cole, come," and we walked back to the house. The older woman who lived two houses down was standing outside, watering her garden. She saw me and smiled. I said, "Hi," and she said, "Hi." Then she said is everything okay, I saw an ambulance. I told her that my father had been not feeling well and throwing up. I went inside the house, and Ma was lying on the bed that Papa sat on doing prayer. I cleaned Cole since Rav was taking care of Jordan and working.

She was sitting on his side and saw me. She said, "He went in the ambulance. I don't know what is happening to him. What is wrong with him?" I stood quiet and said, "The hospital will find out what's wrong and make him better." After a few minutes, I sat on the bed, and I saw Daniel had an IG story with a picture of a stress x-ray. I think due to just wanting a distraction, I messaged him jokingly, "What is a stress x-ray?" He responded, and to amuse myself even more, I wrote, "It sounds painful for the patient." He replied, "it's only 30 seconds long." I giggled. "Alright then." The school year had started, and I remember the week before, I had to report to the school along with the other teachers. I used the time in the library to make flashcards for the second master program I was doing and had a garment on due to getting liposuction.

Thank you, Babaji and God, that I had a short text convo with Daniel. This is turning out or ending out quite a year with regards to investing in myself and fixing myself. Putting myself out there and challenging myself. Just like PD, I am looking for personal development opportunities. When the teacher Corey Perlman sent a staff email that he needs coarpooling, I saw it as an opportunity to be in a place where I am going to work/drive with a guy. I never had that; that is foreign to me, being around a guy & just chatting. My intuition said to take this as a chance to be comfortable & used to something so you are prepared. Babaji & God, I know you are listening and you have a hand on this with me. The hope lives, Babaji & God.

9/18/20

Babaji and God, when I take off the layers that surround the core of what I want, what do I see? When I take off the image, way of life, and Daniel. What I want is a companion, that kind of love, Babaji & God. Just because I never pursued it by putting myself out there. Never took steps, doesn't mean I don't want that. Years went by without it. Babaji and God, don't hold that against me because I am really grateful for the positions you are putting ne in. Walking to Dunkin with a male teacher today. I am 35, and that is a new concept for me, but I am not ashamed or feel less. Even when Perlman said he didn't need a ride home because he was going to the city. I didn't feel angry, like, where is my Friday night fun or feel old. I texted him, "Have fun," because he is in his 20's, & I was sincere. Babaji and God, these positions are helping me & preparing me because this was my hesitation about being around guys. Thank you, Babaji & God.

9/20/20

What have I learned these past 6 months? Babaji and God, the obsessive energy of Daniel is lessening in my system. The overconsume has left my system. I am not saying that, Babaji & God, I am giving up hope because I still have hope for Daniel, but it's not eating me up that I can't focus on other things. I need to focus on work, WGU, the screenplay and myself and my life. It's not that I am settling back into my life before March. I still want to move forward with my life and have my own. I know I don't want Mami's world, and I am not an extension of her. I know I am sailing in the direction of my mothership because I know who I am now. I know living here with Rav & my parents doesn't serve my purpose anymore. I would love to visit Rav's house & play with Jordan & Cole and see my parents. But I can't live with them because I can't focus on my creative craft, WGU, and its distractions with the work involved. Rav isn't going to be able to fix that, and that's okay, Babaji and God, because Rav has made her life and world. God bless her for that. Now that I know I want to move forward, I need to show it and do something about it. Continue investing in myself and know I have all the options. I didn't write myself off & link my perspective to Ma's people, but I found another perspective & invested in myself to be the best version of myself.

Babaji & God, I feel I have completed the spiritual and still need to work on the physical. I learned I have wants, needs, desires, and a calling. It would be wrong, Babaji & God, now that the consumption is out of my system, to just throw all of that under the rug & go back to how things were before March. To go back to the way of life and my duties in this house. That is what I did when the (interest) diminished with those 3 guys, Babaji & God, and I didn't progress because I didn't want to learn. I have learned. I thank Daniel and what he made me feel that opened me to the path of working on myself.

Sim came to visit and help with Papa and the move. Yesterday, she gave me some clarity since now reflecting on how I behaved these past 6 months. Sim said you aren't selfish for wanting your own life, but it's about the right time. Right now, the focus is on Papa, and I should be patient. I did not rush into something stupid and get myself into something because I was impulsive. Trust the process. Rav even said that. Sim said I'm not old; age is just a number. Babaji and God, I trust that you have put me in the place/journey I should be in.

Regarding Daniel, the other day, that female put a pic of his dog. There was an arm & it could be his. I started to cry in front of Babaji's picture. This still hurts. Asking why this (road) again. It's familiar to me. Babaji & God, the crying helps to release. The next day was the return of kids at LHS167. Being around 6th graders who have this innocence & fresh personality helps. To see goodness and their joy to be in school after the shut down.

Yet I know these past days I am walking around with this heartbreak/heartache. Babaji and God, I just feel at times foolish or ashamed that I just threw myself out there. Liking Daniel's stories and initiating convo with a question about his IG story. Babaji & God, I know that was the goal in March to put myself out there, but what came well? I know I shouldn't feel foolish because I took a risk/showed courage & went after hope. Yet, Babaji & God, I have felt this hit my confidence & going to work like I just started feeling not wanted or more of an outsider. But I am not, Babaji & God. With all the work I did & investing in my growth, I won't let this bring me down. I will remain strong & positive. Babaji & God, you know if there is to be anything with regards to Daniel. All I can do is be and trust the process, trust your process, your dream & journey for me.

Why am I single? Babaji and God, I need your help with this. I wrote about this before, in my twenties. Never had a boyfriend or any level of intimacy. I don't know where to start. My parents had an arranged marriage. My mom wasn't encouraging dating. I didn't see my sister's date. Even though I knew/saw Rav had guy friends. I saw my friends in H.S. have boyfriends, but I was not interested in that. However, I wasn't being asked out or approached by guys. My college life was to go to classes, go home, and work. I was reluctant to seek a bf.

I wasn't open to it. Part of me thought my mom would take care of me having a partner. But after graduating college, the guys she told me about I wasn't interested. I didn't like the process because it felt forced/rushed. I tried to negotiate that I could look to find someone in my mom's circle that I naturally was interested in. I found guys, but they weren't interested or available. As time went by, I focused on the things/goals I needed to focus on. Being open to everything in life but close to that. It was fine, I have a big family, and I am close to my sisters. I hang out with them. Now I feel being financially secure and know what I want, and I am open to not having that area empty. Babaji and God, I don't want to be alone for the rest of my life. I want a life of my own and move forward. I know I have built the life I have now on my own, and this is my responsibility. Babaji and God, I doubt if I can just date multiple guys. I am traditional/conservative.

I never was this active/consistent party/clubgoer. I am more of an intuitive/selective person. If I find someone interesting, then I focus on that. Babaji and God, I am linear that way. Babaji and God, I don't know if being that way is going to help me with this, but I know, Babaji and God, you will help me with this.

Babaji and God, what is happening? What is going on? Yesterday, I found out how Daniel sounds. His IG had a post about him doing a lecture, so I saw the video. Babaji & God, my intuition these past few months & even now has been right on. I can say 100%. Through the video came these revelations of things my intuition sensed. He talked about 2 am calls to the ER, not going out much due to studying & residency, his sister expecting & nothing about a gf—all things my intuition sensed. However, Babaji & God, I can't erase the fact that I am hoping with no anchor. Daniel doesn't follow me back, like a post, or start a convo. I have done all these things. Babaji & God, I am tired of thinking about him in all my free days or time on a Saturday. Pursuing him when I can pursue fixing my screenplay & focus on the writing. Babaji & God, what am I doing? Is there anything to come out of this? Babaji & God, I feel hopeless. Babaji and God, I need clarity. I need guidance.

Babaji and God, you gave clarity. One of the things I asked for at the beginning of this (summer). It came from that video, where Daniel expressed not partying due to studying. To me, it revealed that there is someone like me. That's me/was me. He got somewhere to show for it. I realized so did I. It just made sense now, and things are clear on why, with those 3 guys, it didn't happen.

Because they connected with someone who grew up like them, they related to that. It's clear to me now where I need to go and where I need to look. Babaji & God, I didn't understand that you were telling me that I was looking in the wrong place for love. Babaji & God, I don't regret chatting/messaging with Daniel. Yes, I reached out when something hectic was going on with Papa or bored at work or in hope. Some women could do worse.

Using social media to communicate/talk with someone in a healthy manner is not wrong. He responded, and it was nice. I have become stronger and more assured about what I want. The MDs tell me they want just casual, and I respond. God, now I have clarity.

10/13/20

Babaji & God, I am sorry for being selfish these past 6 months. Thinking, visualizing, manifesting, and obsessing about what I wanted while Papa wasn't feeling well & going on this roller-coaster. Babaji & God, I need to stop thinking about Daniel because I need to be present for the people here and around me. My family & Papa. I need to present at work, for my job. Babaji & God, I am letting go of Daniel and all the thoughts I visualized with him. Babaji & God, when did I have him, though? It was my foolishness to think that when tarots say he is thinking of someone, it's me. I am creating soemthig that has no strong validity.

It isn't there, Babaji & God. Babaji & God, it can very well be that female (Bianca). Then let her know so that I can be free. Even though it hurts, and it also hurts my ego I guess. The realization, Babaji & God, that I did it again, what I did with Manav, Axel, & Gavin. Babaji & God, I am adding Daniel as #4 to the list. Babaji & God, I need to be free. I don't want to, Babaji & God, but I don't know what else to do. Babaji & God, now that I realize that I still am doing the same things/habits that I did with Axel, Manav, & Gavin hurts me immensely, hurts my core, and makes me sad. I don't know where to go from here or where I will go from here with regard to that kind of love, Babaji & God. I need to stop and pause about that and not think about it for a while. Babaji & God, I won't be writing in here for a while. Stop the apps and focus on my family that needs me. I know deep down I still carry the hope, Babaji & God, that it will be, it will work out, but I am not going to consume myself with that hope entirely. Babaji & God, please be with me right & be with my family.

Babaji and God, this is the lesson. Living with hope for someone and something makes you look forward to the day and work. I was getting through my day, through work and all the things in front of me, like Papa's health situation, with positivity. Some things did take a step back, like failing the test for WGU, with regards to my second master, three times, before now passing. However when that hope goes, I feel now I am just stepping back to my life, the way it was before March. The feeling of empty, nothing, difficult to get through the work day, but also something to keep my mind off of that feeling. The question mark reappears of where my life is going. Babaji and God, I know my life isn't the way it was before March. I have grown and done so much work.

Being healthy and progressing in my second master's program. Babaji and God, life is not made up of bases. Just because the hope you wished for on 2nd base didn't manifest doesn't mean you go back to the first base. You move on, still hopeful and optimistic. You carry hope for yourself and open your doors with the help of God and Babaji. Babaji and God, I know you have a great life envisioned for me. One that is bigger and greater than I could ever have imagined. I know now I can get there and carry that hope to get there without distractions and with true clarity about what I truly want. Last night, Sim said you need to first love and be happy with what you have right now in your life. I responded that for that, you can't feel ashamed about being my age & living with my parents, Rav, Jordan & Cole. Sim said you don't have to tell people that, but I want to live in truth. Babaji and God, my life is my life. I shouldn't feel ashamed because it's where I am supposed to be right now.

There is no need to cry and be emotional over that fact. Babaji and God, I know you are with me. You have always been there and always come through. I just want you to know that I am stronger for the fact that it's different than most people. Babaji and God, you made me different and gave me my own unique story, and I am grateful. I go out into the world, and my story isn't anyone else's. Babaji and God, you gave me my won story, different than most others, because you knew I was strong to carry it. Even at times when I wasn't, Babaji and God, you gave me more strength, and you gave older sisters to turn to. They are my angels here on Earth. So, I know Babaji and God, you are good. Thank you, Babaji and God, for the life you have given me and the one you have for me. Waheguru.

11/11/20

Babaji and God, I need you. I am so upset, so angry, and so pissed. On top of that, I am a horrible human being because I am thinking of myself, and I should be thinking of Papa and moving. Babaji and God, I can't. The other evening, I sat in front of Babaji's picture and cried. Saying things like perhaps love isn't meant for me. Where I am right now is how my life is to be, with Rav, Jordan, Cole & my parents. Babaji and God, I know that isn't true. Knowing about life and passing that isn't possible. Babaji and God, I feel like I am being selfish or wrong to not want to be here in this home. When once I would want to not be at work/the school and be home. Now, I want to be at work/ shool and not home. Babaji and God, I am sorry if I was too afraid to take risks in the past. I couldn't be impulsive because I needed security/stability. I was financially supporting myself, even though I wanted to go to California after college. It didn't happen because I didn't get into the film program. My life wasn't one where I got everything at once.

But as I sat there with the ugly cry. I said to Babaji that I was not afraid to take risks, but just give me a chance. All this sadness is just how I was back at the beginning of the year. COVID happened, and I saw Daniel on A dating app. The hope gave me joy and I believed. I prayed, and during the weekend, I saw him and that female in his IG story. Babaji and God, that female wrote how she was impulsive & moved to NYC, started a new job & met a great human (him). Babaji and God, I can't believe that one person can get it all at once.

Babaji and God, you are not unjust to give that to others, & I am the exception. I have woke up to problems needing to be solved, like electricity being cut & still having to go to school to take a test. So many moments like that, I tried showing my interest to Daniel, Babaji and God. I have to carry on and keep moving. As I was walking to my car yesterday morning, I just thought about the warp I put myself in these past months.

Thinking about these people, looking at their lives, and comparing, only to put myself down. That is why, on Monday night, I texted that Perlman teacher that I can't carpool you anymore. My quest/aim to understand/see what a guy in his 20's (late) is like is done. Offered, but never gave gas money or said thanks on Monday night. not that I am saying they are all like that. Perlman is Perlman. Driving alone is peaceful, and I just don't want the noise anymore. Babaji and God, I am good alone & don't want to fixate on someone/image that puts me down. Where I have to compare and feel jealous that they have these things and I don't. Babaji and God, I need to step back. What happened? I took it personally. Like an experiment or research study of the guy in his late 20's & Perlman being the one to find out. In the beginning, it was fine, but later, I felt the difference & started feeling inferior when he told me he was going to the city.

Babaji and God, I am just back to how I was with Sonni. The anger, emotions, and jealousy. Babaji and God, I thought I was moving forward with steps ahead, but I feel like I have just stepped way back to that dark place/phase of locking myself in my bedroom to cry. Babaji and God, I know Perlman doesn't see me as an old loser & so does Daniel. However, I don't know why I do, Babaji and God. I am not old, and I have accomplished a lot and I can go to the city to have fun. I have, and I will. Babaji and God, I will go on vacation with someone. I will live with someone (bf &, etc.). Babaji and God, I know I will have a boyfriend and do things with him. I will experience love/intimacy and find love. I don't have to voice it every day and visualize/manifest it every day because I already have Babaji and God, you know.

Once is enough, and it's out there in the universe, Babaji and God. I know I will have those things even though right now I am crying and don't feel so positive. I know I will have kids, Babaji and God, even though I am 36 years old and I am scared/worried. Babaji and God, I know I will be able to create/extend my family. Babaji and God, you have always come through. You have heard all I have voiced. When I wanted to be in Sp in middle school. When I wanted to teach in a school close by, you gave me the job at 167.

When I voiced for strength & the extension, Babaji and God, you gave me strength, and I worked hard. I got the extension. Babaji and God, when my sisters were at the station, and I needed to go to 4th grade the next day to take the state test. You gave me strength, and I kept my composure/calm. I didn't cry and got through the day. My passion for stories & film and Babaji and God, you gave me a chance to take classes at the New York Film Academy. After college, I went with my sisters to the open house.

There was no way I could go to that school. I couldn't afford it and not my parents. I wouldn't get approved for private loans or even my parents. The advisor said Spielberg's son goes here. My parents didn't have money and were financially dependent. At the time, it was the ultimate feeling that life wasn't fair because my parents couldn't help me financially. I was okay with that and started working at 17, but I really wanted to go to the Academy. However, I got to go, and it was Babaji, and God gave me the job at 167 to make money and have the resources to go there and take screenwriting classes to finish that script. Babaji and God, off to those people. To hell with Daniel and all of them because there is nothing to feel inferior about. All I should feel is superior. Not that they did anything or said anything to me.

I was wrong to compare and see my life to what they have, and I don't want to see my life with their mentality or mind frame. My life is mine, and it's great, Babaji and God.

I am not desperate, needy, or less. Babaji and God, the place I am in right now in my life, I did all on my own. There was no pattern

51

to follow or guide someone in my family being a teacher. I got an education and went to college despite my parents having no means to fund it. Knowing that I still wasn't looking or trying to find a gut to marry who could financially support me or marry a guy because all the girls in my mom's community were getting married. I kept walking on and moving forward with what I wanted and what I was ready to have. Babaji and God, you always prepared me, and I am not going to cry the ugly cry anymore.

11/12/20

Babaji and God, last night I did the ugly cry. Due to just feeling down and the word, 36, never had a boyfriend, never been kissed, I was looking up late bloomers on YouTube and writing those words to share as a comment. Today at work, everyone was great, and while teaching, Rosenberg told me how her 27-year-old stepdaughter tested positive for COVID because she went with her friends to Mexico. Rosenberg said she was stupid and irresponsible.

I was just taken aback since last Friday, I saw that pic of Daniel and that chick in Mexico. Babaji and God, I know that was you. You can't talk to us directly, so you use people. It was the full circle and the redemption of you saying their stupid to be in Mexico, and don't be upset, but laugh. It's no coincidence because Rosenberg doesn't know I was upset over that pic, but her sharing that knowingly made me feel better and wiser/mature. Kanowitz came to make copies and joked about going to Rosenberg's for dinner.

This journal is coming to an end, and I am in a good place. Schools might close soon again; they will, and I won't get fixated/obsessed like last time. I feel bad for the kids to sit at home again, knowing that one boy expressed looking forward to being bored, sad/frustrated. Rosenberg said start packing what you need; we are shutting down.

I found this blank notebook as I was clearing the garage. Another garage to empty for a move. Rav has been upset and frustrated due to the mortgage people keep asking for statements and delaying the closing. Babaji and God, you know I prayed for Rav to have this. On the other hand, I got upset/emotional over D-man last night. Rav said relationships/love is supposed to be easy, not complicated. Babaji and God, last night I said to you I can't handle this. I was listening to Shabad and my divine counterpart. Told Rav about D and that he was respectful to respond, unlike the other Indian doctor I messaged and didn't respond. The Indian guy who wanted to send me an Uber, the one who asked why I was on this app (it's hookup), the one who asked what I was wearing, and the one who said he likes oral. Rav said the truth is non-Indian are nicer, and at least I know what I want.

Then I asked Rav if she felt people came to activate you. This morning, I was upset when I came downstairs and saw Papa in the wheelchair. I went upstairs and thought how unfair this is Babaji and God. The story continues with the hardships Rav, Sim, my parents and I have seen. Then I got angry, and I created the scene in my head (inspired by Good Will Hunting). I am sitting on a bench next to D, saying, "But you probably don't know how it feels. You have no idea." SCENE.

I was thinking a lot about what you asked. Why single? (Someone on A dating app asked me that). You have no idea. Your parents invested money and interest in your education. You don't know how it feels to have parents who did neither. Yet, I went to college and beyond with the resources I had. You went away to college and had some fun. You don't know how it feels to go to college and work two jobs. You dated in college, but that wasn't my reality in college. I closed myself on focusing on that department due to the situation. I chose to wait for my parents to make things normal. I learned the hard way and wouldn't advise/wish that on anyone. Anything close to feeling normal was due to my sisters. I reached out to you because I wanted to put myself out there. Really the first time, I can't complain. You responded, but not interested though. I learned I can do this, and it's not too late.

As I finished thinking of that scene, Babaji and God, my hope was closure and peace, but it just heightened my hope. Then the tarot card video gives me clues and more hope to keep believing. When she says you might be dealing with a sag. Then I take Ma to Trader Joe's, and I am waiting in the car. Then, another tarot video of her saying you might be dealing with a libra, and it's a blessing/gift. Then I looked at the egg freezing, and they said $550 for the initial, but when I called, they said the first visit was free, and I could set it on the app. Babaji and God, the moment I feel okay and at peace to let this go is the exact moment when clues/info come to me that keep the hope going. Babaji and God, I looked around the shopping center with Cole, with schools fully remote now and COVID's going up.

My mom called me from Traders Jo, asking what I wanted and asking the associates to help her find these things. So sweet is my mom, and being in her company all my life. I think, Babaji and God, why can't I just be content with all this I have and how things are? But that's because we are all humans who are evolving and need to plan for the life ahead and our life for how things are now changes.

As I drove with Ma back home, I turned at the light and saw a maternity store. Babaji and God, love is supposed to make you feel good and not less. I don't know why D responded to my messages if he wasn't interested. I can't complain because it made me feel good. Babaji and God, I can't complain with regard to anything in my life right? Life is good, and I have love with people who care about me and always have. Rav was right that I knew how to write, so I should do it. I don't need to ask permission. That was another tarot video tidbit that will lead me to be more creative, pour into that. Babaji and God, I need to write and I need to do. No more asking, looking for assurance/reassurance, or permission. Just do it, go for it.

The way I see it, God and Babaji challenge us. If you don't get something you want. It doesn't mean it's the end, and God/Babaji doesn't want you to have it. It's really God/Babaji saying, alright, Harleen, I want you to find a way to have this by thinking of a new path/way than the one you thought. I will give you patience, but you need to be strong to fight the distractions. I can honestly say that has been the walls. Not obstacles but distractions.

I don't know if you know how hardships feel. To have it hard, but to not let it consume you because then you won't have a future (and feel stuck. I don't know if you know how that feels? Stuck? As hard as you try and hope).

16 million COVID cases in the U.S, and that is so sad. Papa is still not motivated to do things on his own, even with and coming. I believe Mom, Rav, and I are handling this at best. We are strong. I am not depressed over it all because I feel what life has done so far is to prepare me for anything. When Lucky was sick and needed his meds and to be fed on time. Babaji and God, I surrender to you. I leave it to you. These past 7 months of turnaround. The schools shut down in March. Reopening got delayed to Oct, and then shutting down in Nov (last Thursday). Through it all, I prayed to you, Babaji, and God for things love and talked to you about Daniel. The communication I started.

The things I visualized and manifested to only look at you. Babaji and God, for reassurance of my hope, love, and partnership. I surrendered because following someone's life on IG is not the only thing I should be doing. While I prayed for that, I should have prayed for the courage to finish my screenplay. The focus is to finish my stories and the master's program. Now again, this is the opportunity to accomplish those things.

An opportunity has risen and come again. Babaji and God, I need to use this opportunity in the best way that suits me and betters me. I believe in signs, Babaji, and God. I believe in intuition, Babaji, and God. I believe in energy, Babaji, and God. Now, when D put that story of the female with Chick-fil-A and the ambulance in the background. There was energy to read there, but it's not my place to say even though these accounts are public for all to analyze, be subjective to feel satisfaction, validation, and important/special. Babaji and God, no one should give anyone that much power/importance. It's the same line, "Why are you giving these people so much importance?" It's the habit that I need to remove, Babaji and God. Giving myself importance is the key.

11/28/20

Babaji and God, I just want to let this go and write it all. Babajia and God, it's not that you are listening to me now. You have always been listening, Babaji and God. I can remember being 10 years old and believing in soul mates and destiny. Someone is made for everyone, and God/Babaji brings that person to you.

Ma thought it was silly. As life continued, I forgot about that, and it wasn't the center of my attention. Other things and goals took over, like school, working, and my dreams of telling stories/creating. The home situation. Unlike the others, Daniel reminded me and brought me back to what I thought and loved when I was 15, what I believed. I lost sight of that. I was looking at guys in my mom's circle. Looking towards my mom to help and take care of that part of my life. When I decided to open myself up and look at other places/options, it was a better response where I was concerned. I never imagined having a boyfriend, living with him in (Manhattan or wherever).

I imagined I would live with my family and move out when I got married. I did look into getting an apartment, but I couldn't afford it after looking at the listings from the agent. Babaji and God, when I saw Daniel's pic and profile, that is what I imagined doing (for the first time). All these possibilities and options that I never imagined for myself opened up. Babaji and God, now my thoughts changed from living with in-laws and a husband that I met through my parents. Thinking that is how it might be for me now, knowing that Babaji and God have a different visions/course for me. One that fits me best and serves me best. In January and Feb, I was praying to Babaji and God for strength to work hard and get through work/the job so I could get the extension.

But, Babaji and God, you just didn't give me the strength not to give up; you gave me a lot of clarity and answers to my questions about where I truly fit/belong. Understanding who I am truly & what direction suits my soul. Babaji and God, if that was Daniel on the bike, then you have been listening all along and proved to me to hold on to those beliefs about love when I was 15. I never imagined having a chance encounter like that where I look at him & he puts his head down and exhales deeply from his mouth. All that has happened (in my life, so far). Babaji & God, I never imagined or thought of it myself. I never imagined sending emojis and messages to a guy like Daniel, and for him to respond was an exciting surprise that gave me joy.

It changed how I thought about what I am capable of. I can make the first step and put myself out there. Babaji and God, I did. I don't have to settle for less. I am grateful to you, Babaji and God, that you gave me the strength to not settle for less. You activated my intuition that spoke to me about what I should do and what I shouldn't do. I never imagined teaching English at a Middle school in Whitestone. All these things I never imagined could happen to me are a part of my life and my journey. It validates that even though. It's my life, but Babaji and God are listening and outpouring at the right time.

In the outer world, the cases of COVID are just getting higher. Such a sad, and in the inner of the home, there isn't peace with Papa being sick & depressed. Refusing to leave the bed. It's true what you think ends up being released at the end of the day. My thoughts have gone to fear Babaji & God. Even though I got educated and am a professional (teacher) with a career. Babaji and God, I still find myself in this cycle, and what if I can't get out of the cycle where I have a partner/spouse and have my own life and something of my own/ I have voiced my desire to move forward with my life and the desire to want my own life. Tonight, the home front of arguing, dysfunctional, and no peace rose again. Ma was not coping with it, and her habit of her ego being threatened and being attacked or told off or being spoken down to makes her react with anger, and she says she will take poison with Papa.

Babaji and God, that scene is so familiar, so common, and repetitive in my life of all these years that I don't even have a reaction to it anymore. Babaji and God, I think my numbness and unhappiness might be all over my face. Michael, the 6th grader in my class, wrote in the chat on Google Meet that Ms. Harleen, you look sad. I told him I was tired, Babaji, and God. I can't let that win or the situation so old win and ruin everything I worked/struggled/sacrificed for. Babaji and God, I can't be in the land of La La anymore. I have to be serious about my future here. Babaji and God, I trust you, and I believe in you. I know you will take me to my new beginning, my next chapter. Babaji and God, where I can truly leave on world and enter a new world. Babaji and God, I believe and surrender to you. I know you are with us all, Babaji and God. I need to deal with/take care of the things in my life right now in order for what I desire to come in. sunny uncle coming to visit and bringing up Raveena when she was kicked out of school. (Jerk) Babaji and God are watching.

Babaji and God, should I make a YouTube video where I share about being 36, single, never having a boyfriend and a virgin? When I wrote that as a comment on someone's similar video, another person replied today that I should make a video. Babaji and God, perhaps this can be the start of the dream/goal of sharing my stories. There was a vision I had in my post. Daniel's no-interest can lead to me doing something creative that makes a splash for him to notice.

At that time, I envisioned an article that a colleague told him about. He communicates with me and wants to know who I am. Imagine, if that came true, Babaji and God. I would never doubt anything being possible. Babaji and God, I am thinking about the juxtaposition of tarot card videos and me doing what they say. That would be quite a visual, Babaji and God. Babaji and God, this is the second chance.

The schools shut down again, and my intuition was saying here is your chance again, Harleen, do it and don't blow it, Babaji and God, here I am making Daniel something when I can be the something. I can have more followers than him on IG. Babaji and God, I have creativity, I have stories, and I have words. Babaji and God, please give me the strength and clarity to do this right. You gave me the strength to take the risk of messaging Daniel and the persistence. Babaji and God, I need you to give me direction on if I should make the YouTube video. Is that the right step, Babaji and God? Please give me clarity on this because I know now where I fit and belong and the direction I should go. The direction of mothership of my soul. I don't want to lose way.

Babaji and God, this morning, I was crying and clinging to your picture in my room. In the evening, I laugh and find humor. I think I have Papa's mood spectrum. This morning, it was hard. Papa was complaining about his throat. He was gagging and throwing up eggs with the aide. Babaji and God, I got angry and upset that this isn't fair to anyone. What did we do to be here or even Papa to deserve this? Babaji and God, I was questioning you and even with Daniel, like why did you bring that profile/pic to me for me only to feel this way right now? In the evening, I ended up creating a moment where I had to get knee surgery, and he was there because he was a resident. He had to get all the supplies. Then it dawned on me that as a resident, he must work like a dog and have no respect. He had an IG story where he was wheeling supplies. I can relate to that by remembering when I was a student teacher. The teacher had me sit in the back and sort folders during Parent Teacher Conferences. Still, the job has no respect with Admin and staff. He must be so confused about why I reached out to him, Babaji, and God. I guess I am the ultimate teacher and encourager and asking him those medical questions would make a resident encouraged and feel better. However, that all depends on how he sees it.

Babaji and God, then I don't feel so foolish to have reached out and asked those questions. It could very well encourage someone in a position like that right now. Then I did a good deed, Babaji and God. I was an encourager and nurturer, and he might wonder why someone like me reached out to me. Babaji and God, from the guys I have seen, there are ones who aren't even intelligent and who are my age or older. I saw someone that my intuition said was. I should put in my tenure binder that I am the ultimate teacher, and I go on dating apps to see who has potential (Lol). I don't need to make a video saying I am single, 36, a virgin, and never had a boyfriend. I am more than those things, Babaji and God. I am a teacher, creative, have stories, and know how to write.

Babaji and God, I am praying for Papa and a miracle. We need Papa. There are so many things Papa needs to see. I want my Papa at my wedding. Babaji and God, I feel so wrong that I spent these past 7 months thinking about myself, about a guy. Babaji and God, praying for what I want, writing about him and my wants. I should have spent that time praying for Papa. Babaji and God, I am praying now for Papa. Be unfair to me, Babaji, and God. Don't be unfair to anyone else in my family. Babaji and God, please bring Papa home to us from the hospital as better. I am sorry, Babaji and God, for being oblivious and not taking in what was going on around me. Instead I created my own world and imagined in my imaginary world with people I never met. Papa is good, and I am bad. I need my Papa, Babaji, and God. I need Papa to know how much he has done for me, and I want to do so much for my Papa. Waheguru!

Babaji and God, I need you to make Papa better and bring him home to us. Babaji and God, I know he got weak, but only 72. There is so much more life to live and things to see. I am disgusted and ashamed of how I behaved these past few months. I wasn't present and in my own world. Thinking about people not in my life or even relevant. Caring what work people thought and the guy thought. I gave power to others and not power/care to my Papa. Babaji and God, I took the people in my life, my family for granted. Babaji and God, I feel I could have done much better these past few months. Instead, there were moments when I yelled at Papa with regards to when he called Sim and wanted to cancel Jordan's birthday.

Babaji and God, I didn't mean it. I reacted because Rav was upset and felt I needed to defend her. Babaji and God, I feel so guilty and so sorry. Babaji and God, I can't go back and redo, but now I am present. I am not going into my own world and looking for distractions like IG profiles, tarot videos on YouTube, or writing pages about some guy I never met in my journal. Babaji and God, I behaved immaturely. Babaji and God, I need Papa to show that I can do much better. Babaji and God, I want Papa at my wedding wearing his nice suit. Babaji and God, I am praying for a miracle. Please, Babaji and God, Papa has Mami. They need each other. They have been married for so many years (45). Papa has a grandson to see and grow to know. Babaji and God, Papa has more of a purpose to be here. Babaji and God, it is still essential/necessary for Papa to be here. You know that, Babaji and God. Babaji and God, please, I am praying. Don't give me anything else, but give me this Babaji and God. Waheguru!

12/17/20

Babaji and God, this morning we saw Papa on FaceTime from the ER. Papa looked good and alert, and his face looked shiny/healthy. I held Cole, and Rav and Ma were so happy. Babaji and God, we never imagined having to rely on FaceTime with an iPad from the ICU so I could talk to Papa. Even writing this is inconceivable that we experience it. Babaji and God, please watch over Papa and make him stronger and healthier. Babaji and God, bring Papa home to us. Rav is right when she says to Sunny that

Papa is strong. Papa has gone through a lot and persevered/overcome. Babaji and God, please give me nothing and give Papa everything. Give Papa all that strength, positive energy, love, and willpower to get better and healthier. Babaji and God, Papa needs to see Sim have a baby, needs to be at my wedding, see me have a baby, and see Jordan and play with him. Babaji and God, Papa deserves to see these things more than anyone I know. Waheguru!

Babaji and God, so many emotions right now. Babaji and God, I feel ashamed, and I did wrong. I know if I feel not well and need care/support, my family will be there. Just like when I came home from the lipo, Rav cared for me. I know my family would do that and not spend time daydreaming of a guy. Writing pages about him and fixating your thoughts and energy on him. They would focus on me. Ma, Papa, and Rav would. What did I do, Babaji and God? I daydreamed and fixated on Daniel. I don't even want to write his name here, Babaji and God. Babaji and God, I feel coming across Daniel Katz and all he is associated with brought an energy that could ne toxic. Babaji and God, I feel guilty. Did I bring curse and bad energy or toxicity to my family by messaging Daniel?

I am scared and have fear. Babaji and God, is Daniel toxic and that is what I said. Daniel and his people cursed my family. Babaji and God, I know that is crazy and negative thinking. Cursing Daniel and his people is anger I am throwing out there. Babaji and God, right now, is not about me. At times, like last night, I thought of him. Went back to tarot videos on YouTube. Babaji and God, all of this makes me feel extremely guilty and wrong. I feel I am wrong, and I shouldn't have done that or should have done all I did with regard to Daniel these past few months. Babaji and God, I can't help but turn to things to take my mind off of things here and now. I look for meaning in everything. Babaji and God, what was the purpose or meaning of the communication with Daniel? Babaji and God, was or is there any? This is so irrelevant and selfish of me to write or think of Babaji and God. Babaji and God, watch over Papa. Babaji and God, give Papa all the strength to fight and get better so he can come home to us. Waheguru!

Babaji and God, yesterday afternoon we saw Papa on FaceTime from the ICU. Papa is off the ventilator. Thank you, Babaji and God. When I say 'we,' that includes Sameer and Bunty, who flew here, Babaji and God, Papa is strong.

Yet, on the other hand, I started thinking about Daniel Katz last night and today. Babaji and God, I feel I have fallen from grace because I felt wrong for ever having him in my thoughts, especially with all that was going on and has been going on this past year/months. I even took the other notebook to you, Babaji and God, to express how I should burn it and throw it in the garbage.

That notebook had all my thoughts/writings and manifestations about Daniel Katz. Babaji and God, I turned to not trusting people and cursing Daniel Katz. I questioned if he threw bad energy/luck towards me and my family. I am angry/upset, Babaji and God. I showed interest in this guy, and he never asked me out or wanted to get to know me. Instead, I had to find out that he was dating a nurse all this time, and she was his girlfriend. I don't understand, Babaji and God, why these people came to my surface. Babaji and God, I know why I can't let go of Daniel Katz. Babaji and God, I am in front of your picture and saying I believe Daniel Katz is the one I will marry and have children with. Babaji and God, I know Daniel Katz and I aren't together right now because it's not the right time. I know why for myself, but for Daniel, it's because he needs to grow more mature. Babaji and God, I know when Daniel Katz and I will be together will be the right time. It will be our time to get to know each other. Babaji and God, I know it will be soon. Daniel Katz and I in 2021. I know this will happen, Babaji and God.

Meditation Mantra:

"Babaji and God and Papa, I know you know I am not afraid. I am open. I am awakened. I want my soul to sail in the direction of my mothership always so my life can have meaning and purpose. I am going to pursue my dreams with love, creativity, and positive energy/mind. I am pursuing my life's purpose of caring, loving, teaching, and storytelling. I want to share my life with my "soul mate." Someone loves me for me, not judge, romantic/handsome, intelligent, funny, family values, family-oriented, humble, works hard, diligent, stylish, swag, accepts me and respects me and accepts my truth, not make fun that I never had a bf or kiss, supports my writings, stories, career, dreams, and forgives.

Papa needs to come home, Babaji and God, and Papa needs to play with Jordan and Cole. Papa needs to see Sim have a baby. Papa needs to be and see my wedding with Daniel Katz. Papa needs to see me pursuing my dreams of creating, writing, and storytelling. Papa needs to see me have my babies. Babaji and God, Papa is strong and can get better. Papa will get better and come home to us, Babaji and God.

Tuesday

Babaji and God, Papa passed away this morning. I had been sleeping beside Ma since Dec 12th when Papa was taken in the ambulance. I remember that night at 2 or 3 am when Ma called me to come downstairs. I felt a chill when holding Cole and looking out the front door, seeing Papa on the stretcher. Then passed out, and the emergency doctor came to resuscitate them. Babaji and God, that image is not my papa. At 5:00 am, Sim came downstairs to give the phone to Rav.

I heard and got up. Ma said what was going on, and I said, "Let me check. I will be right back." I came into the room, and Rav was sitting on the bed. Her eyes were teary, Jordan and Cole sleeping beside her. She put the phone down and said, "he passed away." I started crying, Sim, Ma, and Rav. Babaji and God, I never thought or imagined Papa would pass away or leave us at 72 or now. Papa's presence and a man of not many words. Quiet but sincere and genuine would not be amongst us. Babaji and God, I didn't imagine that back in March when Papa was mentioning his cough, ribs, and chest pains and would want someone to take him to urgent care. Babaji and God, I felt guilt for focusing on other things during the past 9 months. But, Babaji and God, I resurrected and focused on Papa. The past two days I went to gurdwara and asked to please bring Papa home.

Babaji and God, our definitions of home differed. Babaji and God, I got even angry last night at you. I said you can't be unfair. Papa needs more time and to see so much. I can't say you were unfair, Babaji and God, because Papa isn't suffering anymore. We don't have to worry about Papa not being fed in the hospital. Babaji and God, your plan was for my Papa to not be physically near me and us for our future moments. Papa saw Jordan and threw his Lohri party in January. Papa was all in his element at Jordan's Lohri party.

Papa was wearing his suit and clapping near the fire. That was the picture I found yesterday in my drawer. Papa, Ma, and I were at a wedding reception. Papa was wearing a suit and tie. Papa was in his 60s but looked young. When I showed Rav and Sim that picture this morning after we heard the news, Rav said when her friends saw Papa's 70th birthday picture, they said your Dad doesn't look 70. The cats were crying all day yesterday, even when I gave them food. Rav and Sim said they had a feeling. Rav brought up that is was a full moon last night. Babaji and God, you made an intuition strong these past few months that perhaps I saw what was in front of me. Back in March and April, I was sitting in the living room, and Papa was sitting beside me doing paath. When Papa finished praying, papa turned to me with his hands in prayer and matha towards me. Babaji and God, papa is not suffering anymore. I know, Babaji and God, Papa is right beside you. Papa is in a better place where Papa will be out for me, Rav, Sim, Ma, Cole and Jordan.

Papa will look out for us women. Babaji and God, I am not scared of the bad/evil people out there. Babaji and God, I am scared of being out there in the world because Papa will protect me and us from all the evil/bad people. Babaji and God, Papa is looking out for us and taking care of us like always. When I look toward you, Babaji, and God for guidance and clarity, I will also be looking towards Papa. Papa, you are right beside Babaji and God. I don't blame anyone for anything. Papa taught me wonderful things and showed me genuine love. Papa taught me the value of work, love for family, hard work, humor, and being kind and sincere/genuine. Papa is a beautiful human being, good-looking and genuine/kind spirit. Papa was always there for me.

To drop me off or pick me up. Papa never refused or said no. Babaji and God, thank you for giving me such an extraordinary, caring, and phenomenal Papa. Papa never complained and wouldn't want me to complain about anything. Papa lived life on his terms and in the moment. Earlier in the year, Papa said, "You're strong; you show them."

When I was going through the work situation, Babaji and God, I will be strong and show them. Papa can't be near me physically, but he is in me. Papa's spirit is around me, and I feel it. Papa will see our dreams coming true. Papa will see us pursuing our dreams and be there for our moments. Waheguru!

1/7/2021

To my messages, he never messaged me. Daniel didn't follow me back on IG and liked my posts/pics. Papa, I still believed Daniel was the one and would turn around. Papa, I don't understand why Daniel wasn't interested in why he responded to my messages and why did Daniel accept my request. Papa, Daniel played a game with me because he was dating/seeing this nurse chick. Papa, Daniel should suffer. Papa. Daniel Katz will get Karma for responding to my messages while he was dating someone else and not revealing it in his IG.

Was Daniel on the Citi bike when I went to Central Park Zoo that day? Papa, I am sorry that you have a daughter who is delusional and can't let go. I should have acted then in the triple, but I wasn't confident enough. I am sorry, Papa, that I am slow to respond and take action. Papa, I still think of Daniel and don't know what to do. I am angry, confused, lost, and sad.

Papa, there are evil people in this world, like Daniel Katz, who are arrogant, have an ego, like attention, and play games. Papa, I know you wouldn't want me to be angry.

Papa, you believed in finishing what you started. If I started looking to meet someone during your sick months, you would want me to continue until I finish the job/work/kaam. Papa, I am sorry that during those months, from March to November, I sent messages

68

to Daniel Katz while you were sick. I was showing interest, pursuing, and putting myself out there, Papa. Even though I am angry, I feel like writing a mean message to Daniel for being a monster and his family members. Something along the lines of being a monster and responding when you weren't interested while my parent was sick. Papa, you wouldn't want me to message garbage like Daniel Katz. Daniel did wrong; God will deal with Daniel Katz. God will deal with and show Daniel Katz.

Waheguru!

God, you will give Daniel Katz his Karma. God will take Daniel's ego out. Daniel did wrong with me; he shouldn't have accepted my request or responded to my messages on IG if he wasn't interested. God, I don't have anything against that nurse chick. Daniel is the one who did wrong. God, Daniel will get his. I don't have to do anything. I am ending this cycle of writing messages to stupid people. Papa wouldn't want me to continue that way. Even though I still think of Daniel. Feelings and interest are still there. Love is still there, God. I have to carry on. I can't go back and change anything in 2020, Papa; I know you will help guide us to carry on 2020. I didn't get the tenure, the guy, and I lost you, Papa. But Papa, you are with us in spirit and will help me get those two things and much more for us all. I know I will get those things and much more. I know that for myself and our family. Papa, you are watching over us.

1/8/2021

Last night, I was thinking about life's purpose. We all have a purpose to complete in this life. I really understood where Papa came from these past few months. From the things he told Ros and I about his childhood. How Sunny and Gurdeep treated him. In Pahar Ganj, Papa did not feel loved as a child. He fell from a roof, and his father didn't take him to the doctor. Papa came from humble beginnings, and he created a family that cared for and loved him. My sisters and I are who we are due to Papa: professionals, highly educated, standing on our feet, and independent.

Papa invested time and love into us; he gave us everything he could. I feel that was Papa's purpose – to build a family, be close to them, and sing at his Kitty with friends. Papa completed his job; job well done, Papa. Now, I have to pursue and achieve my life's purpose. Give me clarity and take away the anger, God. I want someone to love me. Be romantic and take me out. Make a toast. I saw it on Daniel Katz's IG story with the female nurse. God, I need to stop looking at his IG. It hurts just like a lot of things that have happened which hurt God.

God, I am unhappy and dealing with much hurt all around— Papa's passing. Daniel Katz, I'm disappointed with my job and don't know what to do, God. God, I need you! Please keep me strong so I can find happiness, create happiness, and be happy. God, I need you to remove my anger so I don't feel the world is unfair or that you are unfair. God, I don't want to feel that you take the good and leave the bad. I don't want to feel or believe that the good only suffers and not the bad. Happiness and love are good things for everyone, God.

1/11/21

God, I am where I am supposed to be; I can't compare my life with others. Why did a girl in her 20s find love, and I didn't? It will just put me down and make me question what I did wrong. I didn't do anything wrong, God. How things played out is how you intended God. God, I need you because I woke up a little down. God, I need you so I'd feel that it's not too late for the things I want. God, I need you to let me feel it will all be alright. Papa, I hope you aren't angry that I told Daniel I had a sick parent. Papa, I know you would want us to carry on. You would say your life is still active and moving. Papa, I know you would want us to live our lives and be as moving/active as possible in the future and all the possibilities for each one of us.

1/12/21

Papa, last night Daniel came into my dreams. I remember him talking to me respectfully, rudely to the nurse, and a chick hugging him from behind. Papa and God, please continue to send me answers and messages in my dreams. Papa talks to me in my dreams, giving me guidance, direction, and clarity. Papa, tell me what is going to happen in our future. Papa, give me your advice and words of wisdom in my dreams. Papa, provide me with peace and a clear mind. Papa gives me the feeling that everything will be okay, so I don't have to worry. Papa, I know you are here with us, and we will be okay. We are all okay. I don't have to be scared about anything because Papa, you are looking out and orchestrating the events/steps for us. We are in good hands.

1/24/21

God and Babaji, the other night, I resumed praying since I started in my room and not with Ma. Usually, I start with God, and Babaji watches over Mami and Papa… but then I stopped. The reality is that Papa is not physically here but with you, Babaji. It is the adjustment in prayer. I think of that scene in *Kuch Kuch Hota Hai* where that little girl says she doesn't need to include her mom in her prayers because she is with God. My first dream after Papa passed was an image of Papa and then the word "Meher." I feel I know what that means. Then, the dream of Daniel talking to me and another dream of seeing the word "Jewish." After Papa's passing, I drove to the condo, triplex, and lake. Seeing Papa in all those streets, sidewalks, bus stops, and corners. Every time I see Papa, his face is lit up, smiling and laughing at me, God, and Babaji.

1/25/21

Sim left yesterday evening to go back to California. Even though we know Sim lives there, I can't help but feel that now our family is even smaller. It is now Ma, Rav, myself, Cole, and Jordan. This morning, I had said to myself while moving the shades/curtains in my room that Papa isn't in the hospital or on vacation. God and Babaji, Papa is gone in the physical sense. It is a hard pill to swallow (repeating what Sunny uncle said) because we, as a family, were always intact and consistent despite everything.

From all the homes we changed and moved, what was constant and consistent was my family and us. Papa, Ma, Sim, Rav and I. That never changed, and I am not saying Lucky was secondary; when we moved into this house and Lucky passed, it shook the dynamic core. We helped each other get through it. Papa provided great words of comfort, positivity, calmness, and spirituality to us. It was then when he said about life being chapters, and this is the close of one chapter, and the start of another. We were going to Nanking and sat at a table with an extra chair. We stared at each other: Rav, I, Papa, Sim, and Ma. We looked at each other somberly, except Papa; he was chuckling like it was okay and making us feel better. It is an adjustment for God and Babaji. I don't need to feel desperate, limit myself, or wait for someone. Our lives will expand, and we will adjust. This is the grieving time, and we will all be immersed in the new chapters of the book that is this life. God, I have time, and there are so many things we all have to do, all in due course, and no need to rush in emotionally.

God and Babaji, I owe responsibility for every action and word. Looking at my journals and seeing that I blamed my parents for things makes me cringe. Ma and Papa. They are not to be blamed for anything. Last night, I was thinking about this relationship subject and dating while lying in bed. For as long as I can remember, I wasn't interested in or focused on it. Even though I saw Shreya, Raji, and Ritu have boyfriends in high school. I wasn't interested in having that for myself. Perhaps no guy asked me out in high school or later in college. God, it's okay. That was my reality. God isn't supposed to make anyone's life the same. For as long as I can remember, I always loved to write, create stories, and imagine in my room. For as long as I can remember, I have dreamed of sharing stories. Early on, I knew my life's purpose. God, you aligned my life's purpose with my life. Writers look for extraordinary stories, and God gave me mine at birth. Being born premature into a family with exceptional people, I witnessed their unique experiences. God, we can't control which family/circumstances we are born into.

I am grateful for the family I was born into. Now, this was the past. Now, I am trying to meet someone, and those feelings of rejection at times, I am reminded of God why it was of no interest. It's an energy killer. I am mature and intelligent, but I don't feel that way when looking for or chasing a guy. God, I know you wouldn't want me to compare myself to a 26-year-old and say she was to find and have love and everything. I am not to. God, you wouldn't want me to say that. I always felt like I wasn't kike everyone else, and I didn't desire to be. So, while people look for someone, I felt there was something more meaningful for me to do, more purposeful, and more productive. This was the creating, writing, imagining, and dreaming. Now, I want a relationship, love, and intimacy. God.

However, looking for someone and these apps is an energy killer; I don't feel mature and wise. Only my purpose allows me to feel mature and wise. God, Rav was right; finding love should be easy and make me feel good. It shouldn't be hard, and I shouldn't feel down, God.

I should take the Daniel Katz rejection personally, but I feel that my dreams and Central Park are signs that it should be God. I shouldn't be comparing myself to he is with God; my reality is mine. It's okay because God, you don't intend to give everyone the same life. God, I never wanted to be like everyone, and if you are making my life extraordinary, then my desires are coming true.

1/28/21

Babaji and God, I was thinking a lot about Papa today. Last night, Ma found a video of Sant Sagar and Papa sitting listening to Kirtan. Before going to bed, I watched the video and cried alone. In the video, Papa is his true, lively self, swaying to the kirtan because he gets humorous and goofy. It was like a king sitting in the gurudwara. King sticks out because they have a presence. Papa was not only the hero of my sisters and my childhood. Papa was the King of this family. He walked into a room in charge, domineering, regal, with a presence known and style.

Papa has swag and a personality, which is evident in the video. Even though Papa was sick, he didn't lose his humor, that personality and humor, that personality and presence. Rav said that one night, she put Papa's cell phone near him so that he could call her if he needed to go to the bathroom. When Rav went to bed, Papa called her and said I was checking to see if the phone works. When anyone helped Papa to the bathroom with the walker, Papa made his presence by creatively finding a rhythm and beat while pushing the walker. Papa loved music, but he was also humorous and immediately told Ma to come behind him, making us women in the house laugh. The light and shine on his face with that personality never went away, even though Papa's body was getting slim. On his birthday this past November, which was the last to celebrate with Papa physically. He sat on the sofa in the living room, and we wanted to take a picture. The camera went on, and Papa smiled, that genuine kind of smile that only he could. With that shine and light on his face, with that presence and personality that belongs to Papa. We don't know if Papa knew he was leaving us in the physical sense. Papa wasn't the type of man to start saying his goodbyes. Papa was the kind of person who, regardless of a crisis, hardship, or problem, was the one to maintain peace in the house and keep the same upbeat – that's why Papa was the King. All the people who died in 2020 were Kings, Queens, and other Royals.

No one imagines that Kings and Queens can pass out and be around anymore. But they do pass, and people are left shocked. The world stops, pauses, and things are not typical. (That was 2020 and even now). But there is comfort in knowing they passed in dignity, for they were Kings and Queens – God's children.

1/30/21

God and Babaji, I need you, it hurts. Everything hurts. I don't understand your actions here. Papa's passing overshadowed so many things I was already struggling with. Babaji and God, I don't know what happened in 2020. Why did it happen? The situation at work with the extension and tenure. The hope and wishes when talking to Daniel. Papa is sick and passing. Babaji and God, I am not that strong. There is a limit to strength. I am really trying hard to believe that good and happy days will come. No one knows my past, God and Babaji. Only I carry it and have made it into some shame or embarrassment. I know some women like me haven't had great luck in love and relationships. I don't know if that is how it was written to be or if I am responsible. Monah Singh and others have said to me, love marriage and inter-caste, intercommunity. That is what is written for me. So that is why looking at Ma's circle and those three guys didn't result in anything. Babaji and God, you are saying that isn't what is written for you.

That is why, perhaps even with the job at JH167 (it isn't working out or that issue arose), when Babaji and God have something else written for you, he isn't making what isn't work for you. Babaji and God, I want to be in the direction and path for the life written for me. I can't dwell on the past and let it hold me up. I want Rav, Sim, Ma, Jordan, and Cole to be on the life path written for them. Babaji and God, I know you are strengthening us for a reason. Preparation for something. Practice for me to obtain and seek the love I want. I am 36 years old, and I should not be scared. Babaji and God, I have your hand, and now Papa is by your side.

1/31/21

Babaji and God Rav is right. Everyone has hardships; they just don't put it on social media or say it. I can't sit here and feel that we are the only ones who have it hard or struggled. So many people have lost loved ones. Yes, staying home working this past year was challenging, but we got to take care of Papa. Ma would tell her friends that the girls are doing so much. I can't imagine how Papa felt; he was sick. I am wrong even to question anything complicated. Life isn't meant to be easy. It is about many struggles and hardships. People praising themselves is immature. The nurses and doctors when Ma, Rav, Sim, and I were around the clock caring while working our jobs. Self-indulgence doesn't get you for; you are then like everyone else. Rav pointed out that the best life to live is one on your own terms. You are not just going with what the rest of the status quo is and are truly independent.

Yesterday, Rav and I were worried that Ma watches Sant Sagar gurdwara videos of Papa all day. Grieving is a process; we have to live with the memories and not live in the memories. Yes, Papa left us, women. He was the man of this house for all our lives, all his life. We could never have imagined, but that's life, Babaji & God. Even people in our lives are tangible. This is how it was to unfold, and we have to carry on. That's how we can honor Papa's life & memory. Papa's life wasn't perfect. There were struggles, ups & downs. Papa did the best he could with what he was able & the abilities he had. This is what Rav said. For our childhoods, Papa raised us. Ma said yesterday that she wants to see us married & soon have a baby. Rav got upset with all this pressure of things. Ma feels & questions why Papa couldn't see those things. Rav said Papa wasn't

2/7/21

Rav said how you handle problems &situations in your life is how you are going to handle everything, even your health. But that's free will, which everyone is entitled to. That's consistently into that, and I agree. Papa was independent & progressive. Papa felt you should raise your children, and as adults, you are not involved. Ma's thinking is parent's job is to settle their kids when they become adults. Papa did not; Papa had faith that things just fall into place & things work out. It is how he viewed situations in his own life. When Papa did all he could to fix a situation, he left it to faith for the situation to just run its course & work out. Rav got hurt at Ma because she didn't understand the sacrifices she made & is making these requests. The best way I can explain it is that when Rav said I adopted an image & want an image, I am unrealistic. I feel that pertains to when I thought I would marry someone from Ma's society or even a Sardar. That was unrealistic and an image. It was even more because it wasn't authentic.

No one's life is perfect, but you need to be happy, stay strong, and show them your resilience., and that is the lesson from Papa. It was complex, complicated, and real and produced situations & consequences, which now are closed like the end of a chapter. There is no need to look back.

Once you realize who you are and understand your soul as separate & not collective. It's then you know your true direction. God & Babaji have a purpose for everyone's life & it is our job to find that purpose & live in it. It wasn't just Papa; I didn't even grow up thinking about my wedding. I grew up thinking about being an actress, creating stories & being in them. Being famous and creating so much in my head & on paper. Scenes, dialogues & interviews. That is where my purpose lies. Ma has this list & Rav said to her well, if it doesn't happen, then you won't be happy. You have to be happy now and can't wait for this & that to give you comfort & joy. You have to have peace & faith for what is and what will become. Babaji & God, all I can do is listen to your signs & whispers, work hard, be happy, and have faith.

2/9/21

Babaji & God, the schools for Middle & High are opening on the 24th. It's not like I am scared, but I really don't want to take work personally or get personal at work. I don't work to take work with me home. I don't want to make those same mistakes. Babaji & God, I want balance & peace. I really dont want to invest in something where I am not getting anything in return. This can be a fresh start, and forget everything that happened in the past at work. Papa would want me to be strong. He even said you be strong, and you show them. Being single & working, it's hard not to get personal. I fell into looking at who is single at work. With life, you learn. Babaji & God, I learned that I don't want to meet someone at work. I can do more & Babaji & God, you want me to do more & put myself out there like I sort of did with Daniel. Categorizing work as work will help me reach my goals, Babaji and God.

Babaji & God, yesterday, the professor at WGU said I should try to have some fun during the mid-winter break next week. Forget about the word "fun." 2020 was such a great year that I don't know how to have fun. Babaji & God, I never really did. I can do the responsible stuff. Grocery, chores, laundry, and a master's program or program, but fun is hard. Last night, I was listening to Papa's voice on the voice messages he left on my cell. Babaji & God, I can accept that I won't physically see Papa from now on. Another part of grieving is now understanding that Papa won't be physically there for moments & milestones. I understood that, but Babaji & God, I don't understand why. I know Papa got sick. Papa did mata to me, perhaps to let my spirit know. Perhaps when I envisioned Daniel & I moments like weddings, kids & I envisioned w/o Papa. I created my foreshadowing, narrative, or story. One of them was Daniel coming to our house to visit us. I was asleep, but Ma was there. Papa wasn't there, and now I know why my mind just envisioned that without my control.

If Papa knew & his spirit knew so, he blessed me by taking Mata. Then, perhaps deep down, my spirit knew too. Babaji and God, it's really something. The spirit is really something. The spirit already knows what's going to happen. We don't have to worry about the unknown. We just have to listen and be intuned to our spirit/intuition. It is what prepares us in the best way possible for what's to come. Babaji & God, I can say for sure that my intuition was right on and 100% in telling me during 2020. Even with Daniel, I know he was on the bike that day. Babaji and God, I can't feel that those thoughts, visions & dreams were for nothing. I need to put those on the side & heal/live with the loss of Papa. Babaji & God, I lived for so long with no boyfriend or V-day. I know you will bring me that love. I don't know when or if you already have. Babaji & God, you are my ultimate friend.

You know my wishes, wants, desires, dreams & struggles. You see it all with me. Babaji & God, you know what I want, what I need. Last night, I was a bit afraid about going back to work on the 24th. Babaji & God, I question if I will be able to function out there in the world. Babaji & God, I don't want to act like a victim or traumatized. I don't want to be scared, nervous, shaking with fear, or fainting. Scared to drive to work after so long. Babaji & God, am I going to be able to function? I think back to what Papa said to me after I told him about the extension & not being happy. Papa said to be strong and to show them. Babaji & God, I have to for Papa, but also got myself. Like Rav said, we have a long life and a lot of life to live. When Lucky passed, Papa said this is just one chapter; don't get stuck & stop. Move on & experience all the other chapters.

Just spoke to Rav, and I told her I had a revelation. My eyes have opened on how I act like a child. Rav said you are the baby of the family. I laughed & said I am not a baby. As I was typing the papers for WGU, I was just thinking that now I don't want to go back to the person who went to therapy, crying on my bed like I did yesterday. Babaji & God, I don't want to live my life in default. I told Rav I felt guilty because I remember a course in the summer with Papa where he asked me if he could do the things he did in the morning, like make breakfast & chai. I asked Papa why he doesn't & he said he has daar/fear. I told Papa he could do those things, but he had to be positive. Rav said it sounded like a good convo you had. I told Rav my tone could have been better & that I felt guilty because, at that time, I expressed my desire to move forward with my life & have love with someone. Rav brought up the guy Daniel.

I questioned if I used him as a distraction. Rav said we all do, and I said I didn't think it was to avoid the situation with Papa. I was interested in Daniel & messaged him to show my interest. Babaji and God, I really believed & visualized with Daniel. Rav said I shouldn't feel guilty that life is about who you leave behind & will remember you. Then you are never gone & Papa isn't really ever gone. I brought in logic and said well, I have realized that I am not going to see Papa physically & hear his voice.

Part of the grieving process & why I was listening to his voicemail messages. Rav said you have good ones. Rav said with Papa, he didn't know how to cope & fix his problems. I brought up what she said that Papa's hurdle was financial problems. These are the two words I knew as a child, and I know what Rav means by them. The stress & not being dependent, where you rely on someone to fix your problems & take care of things. Rav did & it was harder last year with taking care of Jordan & working. Rav said how you handle any situation in your life is how you are going to handle everything. I told Rav that during that time, I prayed to meet someone so Papa could meet him & know him. Rav said don't say that because Papa was thinking about his health & not meeting someone. I brought up how Papa told Ma it was good that she was close to Jordan. Rav said Papa was envisioning/expressing life going forward. Babaji & God, I can't make this about me. Your life's beginning & ending has to do with God. So, I can't say I am guilty because of any actions on my part because God wouldn't affect others because of me. Rav said you have to go where it's productive because I have the rest of my life. I put on a dress yesterday, and I felt I could go out on a date; I can do it. Rav brought up we just weren't prepared for those 9 months because no one guided or told us the end stage. Just figuring out, like putting a puzzle together by getting a new piece every day. Rav said you shouldn't feel guilty and see from the person's perspective. Papa didn't want stress or pressure.

Papa hasn't had that for the past 7-10 years. Rav said she understands you're a kid and grow up & you meet someone & get married. I told Rav that God doesn't intend to have everyone have the same life. Everyone is dealt with a hand or something. I don't want to live my life in default, and I want to be happy. I am positive that I got to work from home & beside Papa. For 36 years, I saw Papa every day. Babaji & God, I don't know what's ahead for me. Who is to be in my life? Think of Daniel & it hurts. The hope I had despite all that was in front of me. All I saw

Babaji & God, I am in low spirits this morning. Emotional, negative & down. 2020 has been a roller coaster, and now it's dealing with the aftermath and trying to make sense of it all. In March, with the lockdown, I felt alone & felt something was missing, which was love/companion. I really wished I had someone. I saw Daniel's profile on A dating app and did my research to find him & his family members on Facebook (their photos). Babaji & God, I felt this is it. My someone with whom I felt a connection, Babaji & God, am I wrong? Sim said it sounded like a crush. Connections are built when you sit with the person. I became persistent about having; I messaged him & liked his posts. I kept the hoe even though I saw pics of him with another female. I kept the hope alive by saying that the dreams he appeared in & the guy on the Citi bike who exhaled when I turned to look at him were signs from you, Babaji.

2/16/21

Babaji & God, I was crying so hard last night, sitting on the bed before going to sleep. I think it was a mixture of it being Cole's 7th birthday and Papa not being with us. That was the core & on the surface, the Daniel, Babaji & God. I cried because I felt like a fool. As he was messaging me/questioning me, he expressed that he doesn't remember communicating with me or my messages. He didn't even remember where we communicated. He thought it was a dating app & said people were passing as him. Babaji & God, Daniel is a jerk. Babaji & God, you will take care of that. Babaji & God, here I was, thinking that he felt a connection like I did. He was thinking & knew all the messages I sent him, like the stress X-ray. I felt our story journey had begun, but I only thought that for the past 10 months. Babaji &God, I was just one of the 1,000+ chicks that followed him & liked his stuff so his ego could be boosted. Babaji & God, that is why I fell like a fool.

Babaji & God, I need you. I am trying so hard to go back to when I crushed on male celebrities & imagined being with them. When I looked for shows with couples, I fancied them so I could imagine their love story/lives/journeys. Babaji & God, let me start in the beginning. Zack & Kelly, Leonardo Dicaprio, North & South couple, Anderson Cooper, Jeremy Renner, Vivek Oberoi, Jason & Robin. I even created a character in GH for myself. Tenisha Cassadine, And growing pains, Kirk Cameron and I dated. Babaji & God, I remember it all. Babaji and God, I want to share all the stories, all the stories, Babaji & God, it's hard to go back to that. To get a fill from watching a fictitious couple on screen. It's hard to get a fill when you feel you are about to get the real thing/deal. When I imagined & hoped myself as the one partner of a couple, Babaji, and I wrote pages about Daniel Katz, spent hours dreaming about the life & love we would have, and spent money on all different types of astrology charts. Babaji & God, last night, I am still hoping & thinking of Daniel. Am I crazy?

I did it or what, Babaji & God. It was all for nothing and a waste, Babaji & God. It makes me so sad and with everything else. Babaji & God, I want justice. Daniel Katz shouldn't have accepted my request or responded to any of my messages if he wasn't interested. Babaji & God, I hate everyone, I hate the world, and I don't trust anyone. Babaji & God, I don't feel I belong in this world. Babaji & God, there are so many things I want to do, but I can't focus on any of them because of this stupid Daniel. Maybe why I can't go back, Babaji & God is because imagining is not enough anymore. Perhaps I have changed what to do. To be a doer. Babaji and God, I need you to heal me; I need to feel your love more strongly than ever, Babaji & God. Otherwise, it's going to be hard. Babaji & God, it's hard to get through, and I really make it. Babaji & God, I want justice & peace.

2/20/21

Babaji and God, I don't want to be walking around the house crying like I did yesterday. Can't focus on WGU because the anger & sadness comes; I go into thinking that Daniel and that nurse have a better life than me. These younger people have a better life than me, and I cry when, on the laptop, I see that I wrote how Daniel & our energies met last year. I cry, thinking how I felt he was on the bike, who exhaled. Babaji & God, I cry because I thought you and the universe were writing this, but I was writing/creating it. I feel like a fool because Daniel isn't interested in an Indian-American girl and someone like me.

Daniel is racist, and I am the fool who was obsessed with the younger guy. Babaji & God, where is self-worth? The investigator called to ask more questions last night. He asked if we ever exchanged pictures, and there was an interest for this to be physical/sexual. I am aware of the dangers of social media, and individuals aren't how they appear. Pursuing this complaint towards him being racist for accusing me, I am not going to get anything out of this but to be stuck, especially since I am not completely right. What do I care about this Daniel, who is he? Daniel is nothing, and that nurse, who knows where they will be in 10 years. In jail or another place with their social media, Babaji & God, I have to heal & move on.

I deleted all my dating apps & don't go on to my Instagram. I have to figure out why I cry. Crying while cleaning the kitchen and putting the dishes because of fear of what was going to happen to my life. Where am I and it going? Crying while on the computer because Ma's room has all the pictures of Papa. Crying because I remember how, at the funeral, I held Papa's hand. I stroked it and kept saying I was sorry. Why was I saying sorry? Babaji & God, because I am sorry that in the past, even if I gave any blame or yelled, I didn't mean for Papa to pass at 72.

84

I don't blame them, and Papa was a great father. Perhaps I am sorry that he passed away now & at this time and he won't see the rest. Babaji & God, I don't know when I will get married, but Papa won't physically be there. Babaji & God, Papa won't be taking me to the Cheesecake Factory for my birthday this year as he did in 2017, 2018 & 2019. Babaji & God, I know Papa wouldn't want me to be sorry. I know that for sure because when I would go up to Papa & say I am sorry after yelling or saying something rude, Papa would look down like don't or why are you saying sorry? Papa didn't like it when I put myself down or was too hard on myself. Babaji & God, I cry because I am scared I will be traumatized when I go back to work & the building next week. I don't want to be the sad, quiet, and just getting through the day person. I don't want to seem depressed or look depressed. Babaji & God, I don't want it to be so hard that I have to find a new job in September to have a fresh start. I cry when watching some Netflix show about a Korean-American high school girl who went on her first date with a white guy.

Then, I look up professional photographers for dating profiles. I cry because I don't believe it can happen to me because that girl is in high school going on her first date, and I am 36 years old, not having been on a date. I don't think that an Indian accent with Rav counts since a date should be mutual. Babaji and God, I feel it's too late to date & meet someone. But then I listen to a hymn/Shabad & it gives me peace & removes the negativity, so I don't have to think about these things. So I can carry on at the pace I want and think about the things I can handle. The thing that won't upset me, burn me, make me emotional, or be too much. So, no more tarot card videos on YouTube that just clutter the mind. No more astrology charts.

Babaji and God, I need you. I need you to help break patterns & habits because I fell into it again with Daniel. Looking at his profiles & learning of his family members. Hoping, but the outcome was the same: someone else (the nurse) getting the place as his girlfriend & the comments from his family. I witnessed this outcome before with Sonam & Sameer, so I am doing something wrong, Babaji & God, where I produce & part take in the same cycle & pattern. I end up getting hurt. Babaji & God, I need you to help me be healthy in mind, body & spirit. I am angry at myself. Waheguru.

2/28/21

Last night, I had a dream that Daniel messaged me, "Would you like to live with me in NYC? Babaji & God, I got defensive & responded, why would I live in Queen & work in Queens? Babaji & God, why did I respond like that when that is what I want? I imagined & fantasized about living with Daniel & moving in with him. On Thursday, there was a 26-year-old sub-para & her name was Bella& as Rav was driving to Far Rockway to the school where I had to get my first dose of vaccine, I saw all these signs & store signs with the name Daniel. Babaji & God, I still think about Daniel Katz. I still believe Babaji & God, Rav, telling me to be in reality and what happened is what I created. Babaji & God, this is true that I envisioned, imagined, and believed, but it was supported by what you were whispering to me, Babaji & God, which is that Daniel is the one, and I feel he was on the bike. Yes, Babaji & God, I messaged Daniel after something went on in the house like Papa being taken in the ambulance. Babaji & God, I got emotionally invested/distracted in the hope/dreams with Daniel Katz.

Babaji & God, I still believe, I like to fantasize, I like to create, I like to dream and be in my own world. I don't like to be in reality. That's always been a part of me, Babaji & God. Even though It feels like the world or my world has changed with Papa's passing, I can't let go of that part of me. Rav was right, though the Manjot & Manav aren't thinking about what I have done. So why am I? Why am I making myself stuck or wasting energy analyzing why I did that to them or myself? Babaji & God, it's in the past & not relevant. I need to stop rethinking about it. I guess that is why I thought about that dark day in elementary school. I came home to the condo, and Rav & Sim were about to go somewhere (station) with Papa.

It was tense, and I needed someone to take me to Genovese to get pencils because I had the state test the next day. Sim found some pencils & gave them to me. At night, I was beside Ma & she got the call but was quiet & then she called Baljinder & started crying.

Baljinder came & I saw her walking up the stairs & Ma crying. I went to sleep to wake up and saw Papa eating toast at the table and Ma crying on the sofa with Baljinder next to her. Ma wanted to go see Rav & Sim & Papa & Baljinder said what are you going to do there? The next day, Papa & I were standing in the corner of the House Beautiful. I was about to walk to school & Papa said to me that Ma was going to be upset today, so watch over her & be with her. I asked Papa where Sim & Rav were. Papa told me that they won't be home today, but they will be home tomorrow. Babaji & God, I remember it all. I walked to the 4th grade and sat in the auditorium. Shreya was panicking because it was the state test. I was calm & Shreya asked me why I wasn't nervous.

I told her I was thinking about my sisters because they weren't home. Shreya asked where are they? I grabbed a piece of paper and jotted down "jail." (Great movie/TV scene) Shreya looked at the paper & was shocked. I took the state test & still wonder how I did. I remember when I had my guidance meeting & I went up to her & directly said, "My sisters are in ___." Even she didn't know what to say. She was surprised and said sorry & take care. Shreya & I walked home to see Ma driving near us. Shreya whispered where are your sisters. I remember Ma & I went to the Gurudwara in Flushing. Ma cried & the head did ardaas right there. I was standing where the shees were and the other ragis were surprised/worried about what happened that Ma was so upset. They know Ma & us because we came to that Gurudwara a lot. I stood there quietly. Babaji & God, I remember everything so clearly. I write this again because it is in the past and not relevant. Rav and Sim could have made themselves stuck by thinking about why that happened. Just like I can make myself stuck, but that's not living life & moving on. It's why when Simny brought this up when she would come to visit.

Papa was wrong; it's past. Rav said to learn from Papa that no one is promised tomorrow. 36 years ago, I had Papa near me. It seems long but also short. Papa had a full life with his children, raising them & living his life eating & enjoying. Babaji & God, I will be on these dating apps, talking to those who want to communicate. See if I feel that spark with anyone like I did with those other guys and Daniel. I will try Babaji & God, and I will still think, hope, and believe in Daniel. Babaji & God, I will focus on my career, teaching, my writing, my stories, and to be healthy & fit. Yes, Babaji & God, there is a bit of anger that Papa won't physically be there if I have my wedding and have babies. But I am not the only one this happens to Babaji & God. It goes back to what Papa said: that life is chapters & one shouldn't get stuck on the one that is finished. Papa is with me, and I feel his energy, spirit & presence. When I sit on the sofa & I can imagine Papa sitting in his favorite spot. When I imagine Papa, he is smiling and happy. Papa wants us all to be smiling and happy, Babaji & God. Waheguru!

3/11/21

Babaji & God, yesterday the weather got warmer. When I came home, I saw Ma and Jordan in the living room. For a minute, I thought/felt Papa was sitting in his favorite spot on the soda, which you can't see when standing on the square. Babaji & God, Papa wasn't physically sitting there. Babaji & God that is what I realized that I won't see Papa. I won't hear him say, "Bhar baut aja mausam hai." When the weather changes, Babaji and God, I know I will carry on, but will I be happy? I ran into Vince, the guidance counselor & she had lost her mom about a year ago. She had said you keep them alive in your memories. Babaji & God, I know I can't feel like this loser due to all that happened in 2020. Babaji & God, Daniel knows about Papa, so he should be with me because he is the one.

Babaji & God, today, due to COVID cases in the school, we worked remotely. Then, the email came out that we would be closed for 10 days and working remotely. It's ironic that it was this time last year when the schools were closed due to COVID & we had to work remotely. It was Rav's bday weekend & we went to Toku. Papa was here. I had my IPC with Morris, and the nerves were gone, Babaji & God. She said she wanted to get the observation in before the tenure date, which is soon. Then I went back to a vision I had last year that it was close to summer. I found out that I got tenure & Daniel reached out. Babaji & God, I was taking out my spring/summer clothes sorting, and since the lipo in Sept, I haven't gone to the city. I was looking at the dresses & rompers. 2020 summer was a pandemic & Papa wasn't well, but I went to the city in August 2020 with Rav and Jordan.

That was the day I felt I saw Daniel on the Citi-bike. Babaji and God, since the lipo, I haven't tried on the dresses or tops. They look better now. So much has happened, Babaji & God, these past two years. 2019 & 2020 have been monumental years for our family. Babaji & God, it was the birth of Jordan; Sim stayed here for a year, why I worked in RT (Bayside) in the summer of 2019, the no to tenure/extension from Morris, 2020 Pandemic.

Putting myself out there for someone I feel is my soulmate. 2020 ended with the unimaginable, Papa passing. Babaji and God, life is so unimaginable. You don't know where it's going to go. When things are happening, they happen so quickly. Babaji and God, I know Papa is watching over us. Papa lives in us, and even though that transition of accepting he is physically not here is hard at times, I feel Papa's spirit and his energy. Babaji and God, I have an abundance of memories. Going with Ma & Papa to their parties. I go to dinner with them on my birthdays. The times we hung out and talked.

The childhood memories. I am not saddened that I won't be able to do those things with Papa again because those memories fill me up. Even though Papa is physically gone, I know Papa would want me to make more memories in my life and move forward to the fullest. Papa found greatness in everything I did even when I couldn't at times. When Papa told his friends that I worked a great job in a good school, that I would go to Hollywood or that I wouldn't need to drive because perhaps I would have a driver. Rosenberg had said to me, "You're still young," I do feel I have so much to do. Babaji & God, I wonder what summer 2021 will be like. 2021 Waheguru

3/14/21

Babaji & God, it's really something to see all of Rav's b-day flowers while the plants from the sympathy of Papa's passing remain on the table. Life moves on even if you don't want to partake. Ma, Rav, Jordan, Cole & I had an early dinner at Erawan. Through all these years, lunches & dinners, we are an intact & close-knit family. I was thinking of the funeral and seeing Papa.

As I was standing there, I felt that all of the strength Papa used while he was sick was being released. As I was standing next to Sim & Ma, it was being released to us, and I could feel the strength. Like Papa's gift so I can carry on. Babaji & God, it's like a blink of an eye. Papa was here and then gone. We weren't prepared, but we had to deal with it.

I guess that is what we are prepared with & have experience with dealing with & making the arrangements. With Papa here, it was the living & moving example of my childhood, teen years, and young adult (20's). Even though all of that is in the past. There was the link & connection. Papa, It's interesting what I did with my parents.

As I was getting older I was freezing my parents. I never saw it that way until now. I wasn't understanding that they weren't the same as during my childhood/teen years.

They are older, and yet I was behaving like a child/teen. Babaji & God, I am wrong in so many behaviors. Yesterday, I found an IG story where Daniel is at a beach in Florida. I am finishing /revising a paper for the WGU program. Babaji & God, I behaved like a crazy woman in despair with him. This big dream I had with Daniel in mind is deflating Babaji/God. Love story or story I created because this can be a love story/story. I am writing a story/screenplay here with the Citi-bike & him. Babaji & God, was that the purpose here? I can't take things too seriously or overthink.

That is why I wasn't nervous about the meeting with Morris. She was fair and generous in telling me what week she would come & which class. She said she wanted to make this as easy as possible. I appreciate Morris for that, Babaji, and God. I need to take care of and finish things here. Stop overthinking and fixate on one thing. Categorize & compartmentalize.

Don't get fixated on people & how they behave or what they do. Get the tenure, Harleen, finish that WGU program, fix/revise that screenplay, be healthy & fit, do the work to meet someone and have faith. Babaji & God, this & tragedy feels like it made me jump on the age I am and start behaving like my age or how someone my age should behave. I don't want to act crazy or do crazy things anymore. Babaji & God, it feels good. I am open to anything, everything & all. I feel free, I feel loved, so why fixate on Daniel? Babaji & God, he's there, and I am here. He spoke his truth. I have to carry on.

3/18/21

Babaji & God, I spent last night crying. I was thinking of Daniel, still hoping, fantasizing & imagining being with him intimately & all. I don't want anyone else but Daniel Babaji & God. I spoke to him while Papa was here. I wrote my vows to Daniel, and I prayed. Babaji & God, are you saying I'm not in reality and that it doesn't work this way with regard to meeting someone? You don't get fixated; create images & pray for the person to reach out to you.

Babaji & God, that is how I want it. I want to hope & pray for Daniel even though he messaged me that he has a girlfriend. Even though he has become friends on FB with the cocktail waitress who is now a nurse, Babaji & God, a 27-year-old, is more in reality than I am. But I question that because I have seen real problems, and seeing Papa sick was real. A 27-year-old is not delusional, and I am. Babaji & God, Babaji & God, it was all magical. Seeing Daniel on A dating app. Requesting him on Instagram.

How happy I was when he accepted. Then, when I liked his story, and he liked it back. Then, that continued for a while. When I reached out and said "Hi" to him because Papa was sitting in the kitchen & not feeling well, Papa & I talked about being positive. When Papa went to the ambulance & I asked him what a stress x-ray was. All the times I was down & reached out to Daniel, and he didn't know my situation, but he responded. I would just reach out to Daniel & even write to him that my parent is sick, and your posts took my mind off of it. He wrote, "No worries."

Most people wouldn't write to a stranger that their parent is sick. Babaji & God, I don't see Daniel as a stranger. Perhaps in reality, it doesn't make sense, but for me, it made perfect sense, Babaji & God. Even earlier in August, I felt Babaji & God that it was Daniel on the bike. Who else would exhale like that when seeing me pass by? Babaji & God, Sim once said to me during the Axel & Manav time that I create things. Babaji and God, did I create an illusion or story with Daniel? Did I create something that was nothing or not real? Babaji & God, do I not live in reality? Was the truth & reality with Daniel different from what I thought was real? Because Babaji & God, I thought it was all you, The likes, the bike was from you, Babaji & God, and the universe was aligning signs to make me understand that this is for me to have.

Daniel is for me to have, and our union is to be Babaji & God. I feel I have been tricked, and my intuition was wrong. It can't, Babaji & God. I don't understand Babaji & God. I know that sounds like opera with the color purple.

Babaji & God, I can't continue this way. Watching tarot videos, looking at Daniel's pics on FB, seeing if the girlfriend has become friends with his family members on FB, looking at his chart & my chart Babaji & God, I am having trouble letting Daniel go. Last night, I was thinking about how when I got frustrated and upset, Papa would say not to be upset & to be strong. Babaji & God, I wish I could hear Papa say that to me. I heard him say it so many times: I have an extraordinary father.

I can't seem to let him go Babaji & God, and I don't want to Daniel go. Babaji & God, I really feel Daniel is the one and that it wasn't a coincidence. None of it, and Daniel was brought to me by you, Babaji & God. Even though at times I feel I am repeating the same actions with Axel & Manav, Sonam. Looking at their pictures on FB, the messages, and seeing the progression of their relationships on FB or (Instagram, I didn't follow them there). Babaji & God, I don't feel it would end the same way with Daniel. Babaji & God, I don't want to feel like I'm crazy — even though I have done some crazy things. Perhaps I already ruined myself, Babaji & God. Have mehar on me. I know I was wrong to fill out complaints. Perhaps any chance/hope with Daniel is gone. Yet I still think and want Daniel. Perhaps in another lifetime, Babaji & God.

3/27/21

It's spring break, Babaji & God, and yesterday (Friday) was a nice warm weather day as I was sitting in 167. I walked around the floors because the last period was prep. Everyone was smiling with their small class sizes. Sim came from California for the ashes of Papa. At night, I was sitting on the sofa, under Papa's painting, and just thinking of the memories of Papa and even how he carried himself and behaved while he was sick. Babaji & God, I am narrating the memories & stories of Papa to Daniel in my mind. I am standing at an altar in front of Daniel and telling him about Papa, Babaji & God. Tell Daniel about Papa's chapter philosophy, Papa's greatness, and be strong philosophy. Later in the evening, Rav, Sim

& I were talking about Sunny & Bunty. How they behaved & treated Papa. All the things that happened in the past. We were discussing how siblings could be that way. Have no contact and love. Analyzing Papa's family and how they were raised. Babaji and God, when I think of it collectively, it's a story/journey from the time I saw the behaviors of Sunny & Bunty & Papa's parents. Papa grew up in a family where there was no love from the parents or siblings— then coming to this country & the value being money. Babaji & God, Papa married Ma, and he had Sim, Rav & I. Papa got the love and life he couldn't get growing up or he couldn't imagine.

That is why Ma says Papa wanted to always do for us since we were born; Papa said his parents didn't give. Babaji & God, I just feel everyone has a story with a beginning, middle & end. Papa got the love from the family he created and left a legacy of love. It's like what the speech teacher, Morris, wrote to me on FB.

Jordan won't see Papa physically as he gets older, but that was the story written by Babaji & God. Everyone has a story. Everyone is a story created by Babaji, God, and the universe. Babaji, God & universe give us the ability to get what we need. An example is when you gave me the job at 167.

Later in the evening, at one am, we all went to sleep. I was thinking of Daniel and feeling his energy. Babaji & God, I thank you for what Daniel brought to me in 2020. The hope, butterflies, and belief in love. All the times Daniel came into my dreams, the signs, him on the bike near Central Park, and him responding exactly at moments when I was down because of Papa or something happened. Babaji & God, I will treasure it because it's a living example that the Babaji, God & universe are instrumenting things brought to us that we couldn't ever imagine. A guy like Daniel being a bf and living with him was something I never imagined for myself. A true living example that Babaji, God, and the universe are in control and already have it written. Waheguru!

3/31/21

Babaji & God, today we scattered Papa's ashes. Rav rented a boat in Freeport. Ma, Sim, Rav, Jordan, Cole, and I got the boat and went 3 miles in. As Sim was scattering the ashes and I was throwing the red rose petals, I could see the ashes flowing into the ocean with the rose petals following. I took a video, and it felt like closure of the journey of Papa's life here on Earth. No one wanted Papa to go. We all wish Papa were still here with us, but Papa is in spirit. Ma told us this about the dream she had where Papa was sitting with all of us laughing (kush). Sim was saying on the way back in the car that she kept seeing III (which was the dack#). Sim III means an angel, and Papa is an angel now. Babaji & God, closure has a healing power and a strength. I feel strong and free because I know Papa is watching over all of us.

4/5/21

Babaji & God, when I was on the highway going home from work, I felt I was behind Daniel, who was driving. Yes, it was a fancy Mercedes or BMW, and the guy was looking at his phone while fixing his hair.

Does that sound crazy, Babaji and God? I just felt it was him, Babaji & God. I don't look for him as much on social media. I feel I should leave it to you, Babaji & God. Take this time to finish that screenplay and do the writing. That is the deal I made with you, Babaji & God. Now I'm getting the lipo on the arms & upper back as well. I don't know, Babaji & God. I just feel I need to invest in myself that way. Even though I never thought like that before. Babaji & God, I know you are guiding me, and everything will turn out on your time because your time is the best/perfect time. I take Mata every day with the 20 singles, one for each day. I am not scared or worried. Waheguru!

Babaji & God, what are all these signs and messages? On April 1st, I had a dream where a guy was giving me a closed yellow envelope. In the center, it said Daniel Katz & the address was 44 West or 55 West. It was the office address of Papa, which I saw again when I was filling out Fafsa for WGU. It was stored as a reference. Then, on the left corner were the words I Love You.

The day before, I was waiting for Mom at physical therapy & a guy named Daniel came in. The receptionists were saying, "Hey, Daniel." Yesterday, while driving with Mom after I picked her up from physical therapy, I saw a billboard with the name Daniel. Babaji & God, I don't know, and I ask for forgiveness for what I did. I can't believe I did that. It was so immature, and I prayed for forgiveness. Babaji & God, I don't want to cause anyone harm. Not even Daniel or myself. I am truly sorry, Babaji & God. Waheguru!

4/8/21

Babaji & God, I thank you for the clarity at work. Being able to see work as work. The people there are the people there, in a way. Babaji & God, you gave me something I wished for from early last year. Not to take work home & think about it 24/7. There's peace now. It took COVID & Papa's passing to change that part of me: to not stress over work and realize what is important. Having love, family, purpose & dreams. Babaji & God, I can write a story & book with my experience at 167. I thank you for that, Babaji & God. You put me in the situations & experiences so I can have my stories. Babaji & God, I take mata at Sant Sagar Gurdwara and I write Daniel's name on the note. Babaji & God, it doesn't anger me that he is with the nurse because I know our time will come when it's right when we are ready for each other. To love each other and be the best for each other. Babaji & God, the other day (4/7), I dreamed of the names Edward &Andy. Babaji & God, I believe. Waheguru!

Babaji & God, am I naïve? Since starting this dating app & virtual dating, it seems my eyes have opened wider & acquired this knowledge. Babaji & God, am I trying to believe what is not there? Babaji & God, I feel it was Daniel on the bike that day in Central Park. The way he looked at me, then looked down to exhale.

Babaji & God, I didn't expect that. He was soft and looked at me like I was a star. So different than when I saw him on the bike, which was moody/serious. That is why I got so into creativity & making that YouTube video. Babaji & God, only you know if Daniel is this player with multiple hook-ups. I saw him on a dating app. Dating apps are hook-up centers, from my experience there.

Perhaps when I requested him, he thought I was a hookup candidate. He said he was being cordial when he liked & responded, but perhaps Daniel did to see if I would suggest hookup or something, Babaji & God. I wonder, Babaji & God, when Daniel was liking my likes, responding, & commenting, was he with a woman? Babaji & God, do we have such parallel lives? Can we be Babaji & God? Daniel & I, Waheguru!

Babaji & God, today, during the virtual staff conference, Brent was talking about the NYSESLAT and how the arrangements are behind the scenes. Blake started & Sohini, Babaji & God at the beginning of last year & before that shout-out would have meant something. I am not looking for validation from them/work anymore. Babaji & God, I want other things. I mentioned that if Daniel was on the bike, he looked at me like a star. Today, on the tarot video, it said Libra, be ready to be a star. Psychic said to not focus on Daniel, the person but what you liked about the interaction/connection. Even though it was so limited. Babaji & God, I liked that Daniel responded to my likes & comments &

messages. Babaji & God, I liked that I was interested/crushed on Daniel, who was different from the ones I crushed/interested in the past. I liked that Daniel was completely different from what I liked before. Being interested in him and liking him made me realize what I am truly looking for and what I need. Babaji & God, Daniel brought out the creativity & imagination. I never wrote so much, imagined & created. Babaji & God, I feel Daniel was with a sadar man at the bar. Waheguru!

4/14/21

Babaji & God, Rav is right that the therapist sells the average life. Growing up, I didn't want the average life. That's why I wasn't into meeting guys or dating. I was in my dreams of being an actress, writing stories, and creating. I got into journalism & films. That was the focus and still is. All the young celebrities are focusing on their craft/career, and they aren't focused on dating. Life isn't supposed to be so rigid, and how I am making it. There are so many people who have experience, and I can't be negative. The energy I put out has to be positive, Babaji & God. I just have become so mellow. Babaji & God, it's okay to fantasize. I want to fantasize about Daniel and I. Babaji & God; that is what I want to attract. Yet, I have asked for forgiveness, Babaji & God, for what I did. 20 days of going to the Gurdwara, Babaji & God, I prayed for so many things, including Daniel, Babaji & God. You know, you understand, and it's your divine timing. Waheguru!

4/21/21

Babaji & God, the dream at night shook me. Rav & I were in Papa's room, and we looked out the window. We saw Papa, and it was raining. Papa was lying in a bed. I went out with a blanket and put it over Papa, who wasn't fully clothed. I hugged Papa and said, "Aap hospital jahu. Aap thig ho ja go." Then I said, "I love you, Papa."

Those were the words I was saying in my room in the dark. I had tears in my eyes, and I got up to get my phone. I looked at Papa's picture, and I felt a light/spirit. Papa was there with me. Then, Babaji & God, I looked at Daniel's FB picture with tears. Babaji & God, I said Daniel, you are with me. I imagined how it would be if Daniel were lying next to me in the bed, and I would have this emotional bed. Daniel would wake me and say, "It's okay." Daniel would hold me, say I am here, and you are having a dream. Babaji and God, you know the love I seek. Waheguru!

4/29/21

Babaji & God, I am sorry for emotionally crying. I shouldn't cry because that puts a damper on the fact that I take Mata at the gurdwara. It shows I don't have faith, and I do, Babaji & God, I trust you. This morning, I was so optimistic that Sana Bello had given me the body, and I was looking at bikinis.

Even Rav said the upper back & upper arms came out well. Then it was the end of the day with the students, and I got down like, what do I have a home to go to, Babaji & God? The love I seek from a companion & partner is so intense, Babaji & God. I really felt the connection & the universe agreed. I shouldn't be angry about 2020 since so many people lost and what's happening in India.

The love is not impossible. I will have love, someone to hold and love me, Babaji, and God. The intimacy and my dreams. I am grateful, not pessimistic. You have given me so much. Opportunities and resources. Thank you, Babaji & God. Waheguru!

Babaji & God, what is happening? Where do I begin? Daniel & the nurse had their IG private, and I put mine public. Over the weekend, I saw Doctor Mike's YouTube video about how his mom passed. Then I liked a pic on his IG. Then, an account named Dr. Mark was requested, but it went away. I took a nap & woke up to see a message from the same account saying thanks for blessing my career & you are loved from, Dr Mark. Then the Dr. Mark account was messaging me how are you? You are smart. I asked who this was, and he said, Dr. Mark. I said you are pretending to be someone. Then I screenshotted it and sent it to the real Dr Mark account that someone is pretending to be you. I blocked that account, and the account is gone. At work, I noticed Daniel & the nurse made their accounts public. To see the pics of them that take me back to last summer when Papa was here. It did something, Babaji & God. I felt I was going to faint. Then, proctoring & forgetting to tell Morris about one girl not having an answer sheet.

Then, hearing her in her office, I went and told her. She didn't lose it on me or be mean. She said, "Thanks, Sahni." Babaji & God, what have I done? What I have fixated on is that I can't focus at work. I am losing my way. My mind goes afar. Thinking perhaps that is really Dr. Mark & he likes me. Then I fantasize. Then I think it's Daniel pranking me and I get scared to be on IG. Then I am happy, Babaji & God, that Daniel's account is public. Babaji & God, Daniel's account is public, and I am happy because I feel he is going to come.

Why did Daniel make his IG public? I don't know, Babaji & God. I need to be mature and smart. It's not me or has to be with me. Babaji & God, I pray not to get bothered & fixated with Daniel's pics or anyone's pics or profiles or accounts (IG). I pray for a clear head & strength not to lose my way or ruin myself. Babaji & God, only you know the truth. Babaji & God, who is coming towards me? Mike or Daniel because when I took mata today, I said I want

Daniel. I love Daniel, and I feel he is the one in front of the guru Granth Saab. Babaji & God, am I wrong? I told Mom good luck since I felt we weren't on the same page & he wished me good luck, too! When I met the 50-year-old lawyer in the virtual dating, it had its pros and cons.

I spoke to him on the phone, and he is divorced. Also Jewish, and it was an easy convo. The cons were we aren't on the same page with experience & I did text Rav that I was disappointed that we didn't have the same experience since he is highly educated & went to good schools/financially stable. This has all become ridiculous. This is not how it should be. Perhaps that is what led to emailing the investigator. Babaji & God, it's good the investigator didn't call. I wanted the drama to end, and I prayed for forgiveness & not to harm anyone, including Daniel. Babaji & God, you know the truth behind what is going on. Please reveal to me the truth, Waheguru!

Babaji & God, I have always been a dreamer. As a kid not wanting to be normal but famous. I felt being an actress would get me there. Then, I got into writing and journalism. Imagining that would get me there, the dreamer in me imagined being with & married to celebrities or famous people I had crushes on at the time. But then you have to be real. I started dreaming of wanting to be married to guys associated with Ma's circle. It didn't work out, and

I feel that is your way of telling Babaji and God not to let go of that original dream or stop being the big dreamer. Dreams are imagining being somewhere far beyond where you are in reality. Perhaps that is why I feel I don't fit in LHS167 because I am a dreamer. Dreaming of being with Daniel is far beyond what I imagined for myself. Prior I imagined marrying a son of my mom's friend or mom's relative. I felt that made sense and was practical for me since I wasn't out-dating or looking for anyone different.

I thought it was practical to look through my mom and her circle. Then you brought Daniel to me, Babaji & God, on an app. It opened something in me, the dreamer. I found myself back as that kid who dreamed of being somewhere far beyond where I really was.

Living with a boyfriend and being with someone not affiliated with my mom is a dream I have never had. It was magical when I sent that wave, and you liked it with a heart emoji. A fairy-tale. I asked Daniel what a stress x-ray was on the day Papa went to the hospital, and he responded.

Then I said it sounded painful, and he said it was only 10 seconds. When I saw his video on YouTube for showing Q&A with interested medical students, I saw he used the same stress x-ray. He also pointed out it's uncomfortable, but it takes 10 seconds, and that connection/synchronicity of him pointing out something I asked was magical for me, Babaji & God.

It was like a story that wa playing out, which the universe wrote. As a creative and the writer I am, I couldn't even create or write that. It is why I feel the universe has given me my best stories to write. If Daniel, indeed, was the one on the bike that day, well, I couldn't ever come up with that. We think we know everything, but the universe surprises us. Now Babaji & God, an IG account of Dr. Mark messaging me, leaves me to dream of a possibility that crossed my mind before.

The possibility of Dr. Mark being interested in me. That account might be fake, and someone else might think no way, or it's fake. However, I am the dreamer, Babaji & God, and I dream of the possibility of being far beyond where I am, the real vs. the reel/video. Waheguru!

5/9/21

Babaji & God, I know it must have been so difficult for Ma on the road trip to Newport. For Mother's Day, I remember Papa would always eat at the service station and not in the car. Even his coffee/tea. Papa & Ma would share a BK sandwich or pizza from Sabarro. They had their routine. Ma went on so many road trips with Papa, and we all did. The numerous times to New Jersey.

I try to be the anchor & provide comfort. Babaji and God, I can't say it's unfair because all our lives are written. Questioning anything is questioning Babaji & God. I try to look at the whole picture and how Papa has so much love from us with him, Babaji & God. I just want to live my life fully and with joy. I saw Daniel on an IG story this morning with his family. Seeing him gives me joy, and it's like a familiar connection that surfaces from deep inside: Babaji & God. What is that feeling, Babaji & God? Babaji & God, I leave Daniel to you,

5/11/21

Babaji & God, today I questioned why you took Papa. I cried in the afternoon. I know I shouldn't, and Papa wouldn't want me to. I was thinking of how I would have someone or meet someone. Then I would be on my way and head to the home I share with my parents, Rav, Jordan & Cole, but it's not the people, but that I would be on my way. Babaji & God, I never imagined Papa heading out before me. Babaji & God, I want to keep Papa's life and experiences alive, not to forget. I feel it's one of my purposes now, Waheguru. I will do the wife, mother, teacher, and also the storyteller/writer. I said Papa took a part of us, and I know what part, Babaji & God. It is the child, kid, and teenager. It went with Papa, and that is who I was around Papa.

5/14/21

Babaji & God, I am tired. I did another virtual speed dating, and I didn't like anyone. All the guys were nice to talk to about social issues/current events, but no attraction/spark. Babaji & God, I feel I need to give myself a break and gather my energy. The year that has been and is still doing so much. A lot is going on. Ma is having a hard time without Papa. Then, I drove to the condo on my way home from work. Babaji & God, I feel perhaps I did this.

All the time, I was angry at them for the situation and the things I said. I never meant for Papa to leave us so early.

I didn't want that. It's like I lost Papa not being at my wedding or for the birth of my children. We both lost, and I wasn't that angry, Babaji & God. I can't jump into this whole dating/meeting someone because I need to heal and not look for someone to fill the void/space. Only you know Babaji & God. Babaji & God, please, you need to show me. I am done doing this work. Please, Babaji & God, you bring the person to me. Make it easy because things have been so hard, and I am tired. Babaji & God, who was behind those IG messages? Babaji & God, I know it wasn't Dr. Mark. Babaji & God, I am your child, and now Papa is with you too.

You know what I want and need. Babaji & God, I am being patient. Listening and believing what I feel you are telling me, Babaji & God. Babaji & God, you have always been there and still are with regard to this and everything. Writing Daniel's name on the $11 bills is my hope and faith when I take mata. I have overcome the fear of talking to guys or anyone, and now I just really want to talk to my soul mate, my love, and the one for me, Babaji & God. Waheguru!

5/15/21

Babaji & God, I was watching Selena's Netflix series. In the scene where she introduces Chris to her dad after getting married, I started crying hysterically. Why, Babaji & God? Babaji & God, I am doing the work to be the best version of myself. All the suspicions I've had about Daniel. The dreams and I forgot the deal/promise I made with you.

Dear Babaji & God & Papa,

In March 2020, when we had shut down, I was sitting in my room, and I felt my life was empty. I wished I had focused & put effort into finding someone/meeting someone. At that time, I wished I had someone. Even though I got the extension, I felt like a failure on the career front. With all that happened, I took it personally as if people wanted to throw me under the bus & hurt me (I am getting emotional, but I have to keep writing). I was on A dating app and was open to meeting all different types of guys. Listening to Zully, and I came across Daniel's profile. I searched his name on FB and saw he was young. I swiped like. I found his IG profile and saw his pics. I developed a crush. Daniel didn't like me back, and I should have ended it there. After a few days, I deleted my account. So I am not sure if he didn't like me back. However, I got fixated on this crush.

Morris's words about putting yourself out there were on my mind. So I messaged Daniel, "Hi," but he didn't respond. I should have ended it there, Babaji & God & Papa. I requested him on IG after asking you, Babaji & God. It took Daniel a week or two, and he accepted my request. I was in the room with Papa, Rav & Sim when I got the notification. I went upstairs; I was giddy, happy, and saying, "Thank you, Babaji & God." I didn't know he had a girlfriend, and there was no indication on his IG profile.

When he put that surgery story up, I sent an emoji. It was the first time, and I was lying in bed at night, couldn't sleep, and was bored. Everything was shut down & surgery sounded fun & at first, I was thinking of asking Daniel if they needed volunteers to pass knives. He liked my emoji, and seeing that red heart made me get up from bed. I paced around my room, and I was happy saying, "Thank you, Babaji & God." The indication of the nurse came from snooping when Daniel had a story in June at a restaurant & he tagged his cousin's girlfriend. I went to my cousin's girlfriend. I went to the cousin's girlfriend's IG, which was public & she tagged the nurse. I went to the nurse's IG, which was public, a young & bikini body chick. Then, I went into monitoring & checking their IGs. Babaji & God, my parents had an arranged marriage, so I don't know anything about dating or knowing if a guy is interested. Babaji & God & Papa, I really felt him liking my emojis & comments meant that he was interested. Daniel was interested. It was the end of July or August when the nurse put the pic of her & Daniel in a kiss. I was in the room with Papa, and I went upstairs to cry. I still believed that I could change the situation and remove the nurse. Daniel's coming into my dreams made me feel that I should keep believing. Then, feelings like I saw Daniel on the bike just kept me reassured.

So, I continued to like his stuff. Even the hiking one, even though the nurse had the story of them kissing on the mountain. Babaji, God & Papa, I know I hurt myself by choosing to see that. I am getting emotional, but I have to keep writing. At the time, Papa was sick, too, and sending emojis & messaging Daniel felt good. I asked him what a stress x-ray was on the day Papa went to the hospital by ambulance. Babaji, God & Papa, I was wrong to do that. I messaged him to ask if he was a resident, & he responded when Papa was home. Then Papa was not feeling when & I tried to talk to Papa, but then went downstairs to do exercise. I saw Daniel was on IG & messaged him. Hi. He sent me an emoji, and it made me happy. When Daniel put the pic of the nurse and him, I cried again. This was fall 2020. Sim was here & I had again asked him some medical questions.

Then, when Papa went to the hospital for the last time, I don't know why I messaged him and said my parents were sick, and your stories made me feel better. I saw you on a dating app. He responded I hope your parent gets well. Then February and Valentine's Day, I messaged him. He wrote that he never did anything to show he was interested. Babaji, God & Papa, I did this to myself because I have no boundaries.

106

I expected Daniel to drop everything and check on me after telling him my parent was not well, but he wasn't going to do that because he never met me. I am a stranger to him. So why, Babaji, God & Papa, did I message Daniel as I knew him? Writing has helped to release this. You only look at your friends' stories, not strangers. Babaji, God & Papa, I am angry. I feel like messaging Daniel with curses, but then I have destroyed myself completely. Babaji, God & Papa, I know there was a lesson I needed to learn here, and it was through a lot of pain. I hate all people. I am sorry. Waheguru!

Babaji & God, who cares about Daniel and the nurse. They aren't the only people in this world. Babaji, God & Papa, I need to do. Babaji & God, I got fixated on the pathetic & immature people who have fake lives on Instagram and think they are celebrities because they have so many followers.

Out of the followers, only 3 must be their actual friends. Babaji & God, I am who I am. I don't have a huge friend circle. I am close to my family. I spent time with them when Papa was here and even now. Babaji, God & Papa, it's okay. I have faith, and I am strong. I am not going to get fixated on nonsense. Papa lives on in me, in my memories and the stories. Babaji & God, I felt it was wrong & but it's how Papa said: life is chapters. The best thing I can do for Papa is to be excited about the next chapter, be happy, and not count on someone to make me

happy. Waheguru!

Babaji & God, Papa, all those hopes, visions & dreams I have to put them with someone else I meet, someone who will be interested in me, chase me back and message me as well. Someone who will want to get to know me. We will go on dates, have intellectual conversations, spend time, love each other, be intimate, and go on vacation where I will wear the bikini I bought (perhaps I will wear that before a bf). Babaji, God & Papa, we can then live together & build a commitment. Talk about our future and dreams and support each other. He will support me, and I will support Babaji & God, Papa. Babaji & God, I am sorry that I question why you didn't have Daniel reach out or be interested.

Then I got angry. Babaji/God, I said I will embrace & be grateful for what you bring my way. I didn't do that all the time & I am sorry, Babaji & God. Yesterday, I didn't cry over Daniel, but I cried after I took Mata at Gurudwara. When I went to get parshad, the man asked if mummy & daddy speak Punjabi. I said no, and mummy is from Lucknow. He asked if Daddy was from Delhi.

I said, "Yeah." When I got into the car, I thought perhaps I should have told him about Papa. Then I started crying while driving, Papa, Babaji & God. Then, at the red light, I checked my phone and saw I passed task 2 for WGU. That was you, Babaji, God & Papa, to say you are all with me. Babaji, God & Papa, I have done dating apps & virtual speed dating. I don't know what to do next with regard to meeting someone. Babaji, God & Papa, how do I meet someone? I can't look at others and compare or put myself down about why these people were to meet, and I wasn't. They are lucky & I am not. I can't do that. I am lucky, Babaji, God & Papa. Waheguru!

Babaji, God & Papa, I had a dream this morning. It was dark, and I was outside walking with Sim & Rav. Sim was in a mood, and I started yelling at her. I said, "Papa, you met Jordan, but he is not going to meet my guy/person." I got emotional, and Sim stood there quietly. Babaji, God & Papa, it was a dream, and in reality, Sim would have said something to console me. I woke up laying in bed and just thinking, "Why." Babaji, God, when will you bring my soulmate, companion to me? I started crying, and soft tears rolled out. Yes, it's not fair, but I know Papa wouldn't want me to be angry at God especially. I was watching my favorite episode of Beverly Hills: Dylan's father's death & ER with Greene's death. Perhaps this was already foreshadowed for me to know this would happen. Perhaps that is why I was able to be so strong at work with 6Al talking about death & wanting to see a dead person. I am strong, I am a Sahni, Babaji, God, Waheguru! Babaji, God, my question is, when will you bring him to me?

Purpose: creative projects, writing stories, screenplay (not having a bf, guy, husband)

Emotional Dreams: having a loving companion, family, and children.

Babaji, God & Papa, what I know is that I want to write the stories and the screenplays. I want to get recognized for that and get awards. Yes, it was on my mind that if I met someone who makes more money, I could focus on that full-time. Yes, leave the teaching, but after this school year. I learned I like my job at LHS167. It became a retreat. In life, you can only save yourself. No one else is going to save you. So, I will have my job/career as an educator at 167 and pursue my other passions of writing, creating, and storytelling. I don't want to be in a situation where I am with someone, and I can't do that. Waheguru!

I cried while listening to the song of Dylan's father's funeral. This has nothing to do with Daniel. But today, I didn't know I would write my stories. Papa's stories, Ma, Rav, & Sim. I feel I will get the recognition/fame I always desired. Babaji, God & Papa, you have dreamt a bigger dream for me than I could ever imagine. Waheguru!

6/6/21

Babaji, God, & Papa, these are the plans for now. Finish the WGU program by the end of June. Start writing the stories and screenplays and finish the Ruby screenplay. Pray and manifest for a loving soulmate and companion to come my way. Build and invest in a commitment and start a family of my own with children. Continue working as an educator, and once done with the WGU program, my salary will go up. Continue working as an educator and pursue my passions & purpose of creating, & writing stories. Babaji, God & Papa, these are the plans for now. I am going to focus on what is in front of me and not get myself distracted. Babaji, God & Papa, please remove the distractions. Please give me the strength to not resort to distractions and look at people I have never met's IG accounts. Please remove my obsessive quality, Babaji, God &Papa.

Waheguru! Waheguru! Waheguru!

6/9/21

Babaji, God & Papa, yesterday was the great news that Rav got her house. Her offer was accepted, and I am happy for her. Babaji & God, you know, even during the time we lived in the triplex, I asked to give Rav everything she wanted and more because she is an unselfish person. I remember when Rav told me about Jordan, I ran to your picture, Babaji & God, in my room, overjoyed, over happy, and thanking you for giving Rav this. At that time in May 2019, there was nothing I wanted for myself, & I was overjoyed for Rav, but this time, I didn't run to your picture, Babaji & God.

I walked, and this time, I did want something for myself. Babaji, God & Papa. Babaji, God & Papa, my hope isn't gone.

My Vishwas isn't gone. The prayers, matas, writing Daniel's name on the bills, the signs & dreams, Babaji, God & Papa can not/will not go in vain. Babaji, God & Papa, I also did mata and wrote on the bills to give Rav her house. The power of prayers is strong, Babaji, God & Papa. Babaji, God & Papa, I wrote vows. Babaji, God & Papa, you need to show me all those signs, dreams, the connection & familiarity I felt, feeling that it was Daniel on the bike that day in Central Park. Babaji, God & Papa, you need to show me that it is something and not something I created, but you had a hand in Babaji, God & Papa. The overjoyed feeling I had when I came to your picture after finding out about Jordan.

6/13/21

Babaji, God & Papa, I remember, Papa, all the experiences with you are now stories. I remember the stories you shared and your beliefs so that I could understand. Papa, you were great that way. You would bring yourself to my level. I remember when you got upset that I was cutting my hair in high school. Rav opened the can of worms because I said something about. Papa, you and Ma came up to me and looked at my hair. Papa, you light-slapped me.

Then got furious and said what is going on in this house? Papa, you started talking about religion and that this is our religion. Then, Papa, you calmed down and told me how, in this country, your friends told you to cut your hair because you are in America and not India. That it's okay, and you said no, Papa, because this is my religion. I understood you were under my peer pressure. Babaji & God, I need to share these stories. Waheguru!

6/14/21

Thank you, Babaji, God & Papa. Today, I got the hard copy of my observation from Morris. Two are highly effective, and I am happy. I passed Task 3 of the WGU program. I am happy. Babaji, God & Papa, I am grateful for all the things you bring my way. I appreciate all the fruits and things you bring my way. I embrace them all with gratitude. Babaji, God & Papa, what I couldn't do before, I have learned to do now. Waheguru!

6/17/21

Yesterday, Babaji & God & Papa I came home from work, and I fell asleep. The weather was getting warmer, and seeing that I had dressed, I tried on the one-shoulder dress & showed Rav. Towards the evening, I looked at your picture, Babaji & God, & felt centered emotionally. I had no convo with Rosenberg about Areliquin (Para whose terminal and about now everyone has to go. Rosenberg said so). Babaji & God, I said, with Papa passing, perhaps also the make-believe, imagining, creating & dreaming in me passed too. I questioned Babaji & God & Papa that perhaps I imagined the guy who exhaled on the bike when I went to Central Park Zoo with Jordan, Babaji, God & Papa. There was a guy on a bike, but maybe it wasn't Daniel & when I looked towards him, maybe he didn't exhale Babaji & God. Perhaps I created, imagined, or envisioned that to feel like this is a sign; why did I dream of Daniel during that time? Babaji, God & Papa, when I went to bed, I put it to rest.

I watched a tarot video that my soulmate was there, but it was divine timing because we both needed to be ready. I liked what the lady said about investing in yourself; it doesn't mean the outcome is to get a man/guy. You do it for yourself. She also said the guy for you is your soulmate & a past-life connection. Babaji, God & Papa, I feel his energy at 3 am & 5 am. It wakes me up &, at times, he has put a story up or not. I feel Daniel's energy,

112

Babaji, God & Papa, when I wrote these manifestations/vision boards, it was raining hard at night. Papa, you love the rain. Then the door of the bedroom opened. I feel it was a sign that the door to the love/personal is opening up. I swear, in the dark hallway, I saw Daniel standing, Papa. I am not scared. I am not afraid. I am open to embracing anything that comes my way. God, you are with me. Papa, you are with me.

7/5/21

Babaji, God & Papa, Nuvpreet & Gurvir came for dinner with their kids. Nuvpreet, I saw him in middle school & him getting married & having kids. Papa isn't here physically, but it was that same feeling when they came for dinners when you were here, Papa. Then I think how redundant. God, Babaji, & Papa, when is my life going to change? When am I going to find love, my soulmate & companion? I believe it will happen, but I am getting restless. God, you know what I want, Babaji, Papa.

7/9/21

Babaji, God & Papa, it was the environment, situation, and atmosphere. In March 2020, I was sitting in this room, and I felt lonely. COVID and the shutdown of work led me to reevaluate how I gave so much focus to the drama at the school. Why didn't I focus more consistently/seriously/actively on my personal life? Morris's words, "It's good you are putting yourself out there," triggered me. In 4 words, she knew my biggest issue, which I didn't realize. When someone outside your family/inner circle says something you least expect, it triggers you. Babaji, God & Papa, that night when Sim & Rav were in the room & I saw Daniel's profile on A dating app. I swiped him, and then there was another guy.

He was Italian-American & when I saw his IG account, he had posted that his father had passed away. Babaji & God, that was your way of indicating/foreshadowing what was to happen in 9 months. The most powerful was that late night in bed & Daniel put that story of him in an elevator after completing his first 10-hour surgery. That picture really reflected Daniel's energy, Babaji & God. I felt it, and I asked God & Babaji if I should comment. I felt God & Babaji saying yes, so I did. I went & laid down. I felt I shouldn't have sent the applaud emoji because I thought negatively and that I would be disappointed (like in the past). But then I got the notification that Daniel liked my emoji, and I saw the red heart. That did something to me. That night, I felt so connected to God & Babaji because I felt he was by my side as overjoyed as I was when I saw that red heart. To be honest, Daniel looked good in his scrubs, partial chest hair and in the dimly lit elevator.

Babaji, God & Papa, I knew Daniel was on the mountain with the nurse because she put it up on her IG story. Yet I liked his story where she was absent. (That day when Papa was in the kitchen). I can understand now that I made Daniel out to be how I wanted/needed at that time. The energy I can turn to so I can feel better. One day, when Papa was in the kitchen and kind of down, I tried to make Papa positive by saying to think positively.

It didn't work, and I went downstairs to do the treadmill, but I ended up kind of down. I sat on the floor, and I went to IG. Daniel was on, and I messaged him, "Hi." I had that fear afterward, but then Daniel responded with a wave emoji. I started laughing and did 30 minutes on the treadmill. God & Babaji, it was you not letting me be disappointed & perhaps you did that through Daniel. I didn't see Daniel, God & Babaji. I wished, I prayed in the gurdwara, I hoped and did all I could for Daniel. Perhaps you shouldn't be praying for someone. God & Babaji, Daniel, in the figure & way I saw, was your way to protect me from sinking into a deep hole because I wasn't emotionally prepared to handle the situation. I remember during the hard times I would escape to the other room and listen to music on the Walkman.

Babaji & God, I broke down when I saw the nurse put the pic of Daniel & her. Papa was in the room with me, and I went upstairs. I was hurt and felt it was unfair with the signs and dreams, and I felt Daniel was the one on the bike exhaling that day in Central Park.

Only you know, Babaji & God. All I know is you, and Papa wouldn't want me to cry anymore over Daniel. What is written for our lives will be revealed because I strongly believe everything is already written by God & Babaji. Waheguru!

7/16/21

Babaji, God & Papa, and Sim were crying on the phone today with Ma & me. Sim was sad that Papa just left us. Babaji & God, it's hard to feel enthusiastic about life at times. Being in this home where Papa lived & was with us. With Papa not here, it's hard not to think it's all over & the end. I know Papa wouldn't want that for us to feel life is over & it's the end because Papa is gone. Papa talked about chapters, and this is one chapter.

There are so many more chapters to live through. Babaji. God & Papa, I was consoling Sim to feel better, but I struggled & got down at times. It's like this given up sense towards wanting to do anything. Just lay on the side of the sofa that Papa used to sit on. The missing never goes away. You live with it and carry it with you, Babaji, God & Papa. Waheguru!

7/20/21

Babaji, God & Papa surround me with people & energy that help me to serve my purpose in this life of mine. Please don't allow me to give power to people where I feel down because they aren't in contact with me. Ma's society and Daniel. My soul is always sailing in the direction of my mother's ship. I don't want to be surrounded by energy that isn't relevant to my life and hinders me from being productive.

Every minute is precious because life is short, and there is so much to do. I want to live my life with zest and zeal and how life is meant to be lived. Babaji, God & Papa put me on the course of meeting my partner and soulmate, having my children, writing my stories, and creating and teaching. Please give me the strength not to destroy myself. Forgive me & let me forgive myself. Waheguru!

7/24/21

Babaji & God, it was also the situation & circumstances. COVID, the pandemic, the shutdown, and Papa being sick that birth this desire/wish/belief. I thought I would date Daniel, and I wanted to be out there as I imagined myself. Which is skinnier, so I got on a diet, exercised, lost weight, and got Sono Bello. Coming across that Daniel had a girlfriend. Papa's passing has had a profound effect on me, such that I know I can't go back to how I was before March 2020, Babaji & God.

However, today, I started looking again at Oscar speeches and film interviews at Simdance & other festivals like I used to before I got obsessed with things not working in my favor. Obsessed with trying to change the narrative/outcome with regard to Daniel & Papa through prayers, hoping, believing, & having faith. Babaji & God, I feel that is what you would want me to do. Clear the way to focus on writing my stories, looking at film writers' interviews on YouTube instead of looking at Tarot card videos for Zodiac signs. So, I have cleared my way so I can focus on just that: Babaji & God.

Not obsess over meeting someone only. I know it should be a focus, but it shouldn't be an obsession because then I don't feel good. When I tried to find & wait for someone to come and erase the hurt, anger, and sadness from the grief of losing/missing Papa, I only felt disappointment. Babaji & God, I don't want to put myself in that position again. You can't find something or someone to erase the emotions. You have to walk through them and with them, until they become less heavy, which they do and are now.

Babaji & God, I have cleared my path. So I can focus on the essentials and my passions/dreams. My job in Summer Rising, my career as an educator, and ensuring my tenure, focus on my passions/dreams of writing my stories and surround myself with that. Babaji & God, I believe that writing is my life purpose, but I have come to learn that we can have many purposes to come when it's not the time. We have to be patient and not angry when it's not on our lap. You have to flow with what you can control and not be upset with what you can't control. I can listen & understand that because my relationship & connection became stronger this past year with you, God & Babaji. Waheguru!

7/26/21

Babaji & God, I remember my last year at Queens College, and we lived in the Triplex. Rav came into my room because I needed to buy my graduation gown from the bookstore. So we started looking around my room for books I could sell back. It became comical because Rav started grabbing any book she saw, and I had to tell her that those weren't college textbooks.

I joked with her by saying, "Let's sell anything, whatever we can." I know, for others, it sounds like a bitter story, but I look at that moment & so many like that fondly. Babaji & God, it has made me who I am. I am strong, and I know how to carry on. Make light of tough/difficult situations and keep standing in them. Recently, I have lost touch with that and lost my way & sense of me. I became weak & angry, Babaji & God. I don't want to be that way anymore; I want to remember all the moments/memories. Waheguru!

Babaji & God, I can do Middle School Math. Today, I was teaching the EUS at Bleeker for Summer Rising. I got the answer correct. I think of my time at Reading Town, and working there for close to 10 years has made me a pro in teaching summer school or teaching anything. I was happy when the screen said, "Nice work," when converting the expression into standard form or decimal.

When realizing I could do the math, I thought of Papa in that classroom. Papa could do math without a calculator. Papa excelled in math, and perhaps that is where I get it from. I remember my first year at 167. Maddox asks Chan how he got the answer for the math problem because she got it wrong. I got it correct, and I was trying to chime in on how to solve it, but Chan was worried since he is the math guy. Papa is with me, Babaji & God. Waheguru!

Babaji, God & Papa, I had a dream last night. It took place in the basement of the triplex. Papa was there, and he was wearing a white Polo shirt with a red turban. Papa asked me to help him find something (his clothes). Papa was all in his element, looking all over the basement and complaining about where is it, in his mood. I was looking through the totes & crying deeply because I was thinking how I knew Papa was going to pass & the clothes would be left.

I could feel Papa's energy like he was with me, and it felt so real knowing how it felt to be around Papa. It was like Papa never went away. I woke up, and I could feel the crying emotions, and then I thought of Daniel. In a flash, his face appeared with a white button-down shirt on. Daniel was worried, and he held my face and then hugged me. He said, "I'm here," and "It's okay." Babaji, God & Papa, why do I just instantly go to Daniel? In a flash, his face appears, and he is comforting me.

Then, the image of laying in bed and Daniel next to me. I am crying due to the dream, and Daniel is consoling/comforting me. I try to stop my mind from going there by changing the image in my head back to the dream with Papa in the basement of the triplex. However, I couldn't, Babaji, God & Papa, because I was crying in that basement while feeling Papa's presence & energy and helping him find his clothes. So I went to one where I was laying in that bed & I told Daniel the story of when Papa came upstairs from the car to the condo. Rav & I were in the living room, and Papa was stern with his black winter jacket. Papa threw the comb he was looking for across the living room. Rav & I backed slowly because Papa was mad. I told Daniel that Papa hated it when things were not in the right place because then Papa wouldn't be able to find what he needed.

After all, it wasn't where it was supposed to be, like hair combs, scotch tape, pens, & scissors. I finish telling Daniel this, and he is listening. Daniel responds, "It sounds like your Dad was very structured," while holding my hand. Then I told Daniel how, after throwing the comb, Papa turned around & went to the car where Ma was waiting. Then Rav & I look at each other and say, "Where did Papa throw the comb?" We looked around the living room to see where the comb landed to make sure we put it in the right place or else.

Babaji, God & Papa, I am dreaming/imagining telling Daniel all of this. Then I wake up to get my phone to look at his profile pic to say I feel your energy, Babaji, God & Papa. Why? Daniel has IG blocked me. How on earth will he reach out to me? However, I know Babaji, God & Papa, there is a higher power and higher force that is bigger than all of us. He makes things happen and is responsible for all. I believe that because I think about when I was born. As a baby, I didn't know the risks of premature, underweight, incubators, and lungs not being fully developed. Babaji & God, you knew and stood by my side. God & Babaji told my spirit to gift. Rav had Jordan's second birthday today at Adventure Land. Jordan had fun. I wish Jordan all the blessings in life. Waheguru!

119

Babaji, God & Papa, what was this dream I had just now? It starts with me on a beach boardwalk like Fountain Bleu. Then I saw Brent, and I asked if she brought both boys. She said, no, only one, and I joked the other one was upset as he didn't get to go to Florida. But Brent has three boys, I believe. Then there is this huge wooden floor & her son is there. I am coming with a small black dog, & I put the dog down on the wooden floor where they are running. Then I am looking at Brent, who is an associate, ringing me up because I want to purchase a boat ride for 80 minutes. I am in Florida, and Rav comes with Cole. It comes up that it's Mother's Day, and that would be nice. Then I see Daniel. We are indoors, and he has dark blue scrubs on. He says, "You're ready?" "Let's go." Then, on that beachfront, he is standing next to me. Then, I believe his mom appeared. Then I said to myself that I was in Florida with my boyfriend's family, and it was Mother's Day. Then, the image of Cole doing harkat in our bedroom in the condo doesn't make sense. Babaji, God & Papa, these dreams. Waheguru!

8/8/21

Babaji, God & Papa, I understand now. Because I cleared my path, I am back to my purpose. Babaji, God & Papa, I want to write. I grew up writing. The plan was to have teaching as a secure paying job so that I could pursue my talent. Babaji & God, you have given me that now with 167 for the past 4 years. Every time I get the sense of going to IG or tarot, I will not; instead, I will write. Babaji, God & Papa, what I became with regard to Daniel is a person who has fallen from grace because I am not following my passion, purpose, and talent. Babaji & God, you know I grew up not caring about love, & on the subway back from Jaya Lakshmi, I was 23 years old, and I said to Rav that I see myself as the writer and not mom. I lost sight of that, and it's because I stopped thinking about the talent and the past.

Babaji, God & Papa, I have grown since 23 years old. I do want children, and that is why I want someone. Not entirely, because I want intimacy and a companion to encourage, support, & share dreams with. Right now, the writing is more passionate more of the focus because Daniel's fixation has lessened. It wasn't mutual & he has a gf. That doesn't make me angry, but what does is that I wrote vows & wrote so much about him. My writing is very personal & precious to me, so if I feel it was wasted, then that angers me. Your life purpose aligns with the direction & experiences of your life. Babaji, God & Papa, I thank you for putting me in the position where I didn't have to look for stories because you made them part of my life with my family. I have to let go of Daniel because if he isn't the one, then the one won't be drawn since I didn't clear the path. Waheguru!

8/11/21

Babaji, God & Papa, tomorrow is the last of Summer School at Bleeker. The six-week program has wrapped. The E11 kids were great, and teaching them just reminded me of all the summers working at Reading Town (9 summers) and for POE (3 summers: 2017, 2018, 2021). I feel like a senior or pro. I have realized now that I have to let go of habits & behaviors that I cling to. Working at RT for the summer was essential because it was paid by the hour. I have a career now and a salary now. The days of working as many hours as you can get are gone. The dire financial and money problems are gone. Babaji, God & Papa, I have room in my life now to focus on myself, focus on building my personal life, and relax/enjoy, but it's a habit I don't know. The only habit I know is to work. I work in the summer & do summer school because I am used to it. I forget it's not dire anymore. Having free time is not a habit. Waheguru!

Babaji, God & Papa, yesterday was the last day of the summer school. With the 12 years of teaching summer school or summer enrichment programs, I want to retire from teaching summer school. Babaji, God & Papa, I want to be on my honeymoon next summer (2022) and work on making/creating my babies/children. I cried this morning, and I don't want to go into it. Babaji, God & Papa, I know you see my tears and know all the feelings I go through. Babaji, God & Papa, I know you are with me. Waheguru! Babaji, God & Papa, my intuition was so strong & head-on. The day of Central Park Zoo, that morning before leaving, I was nervous/anxious because my intuition knew/felt I would see him, but, Babaji, God & Papa, was it Daniel on the bike? He had the dog story, which I liked in the car while going there. Now the intuition is gone, Babaji, God & Papa. Waheguru! Nothing is clear. I don't know anything.

Babaji, God & Papa, I really don't know what to do. I don't know what I want anymore. I thought I did. I really did want that and thought it was for me. It blew up in my face and blindsided me. It went in a different direction, and I became a train wreck. I did things where I was embarrassed & ashamed. I am not crying over it anymore, but I am just whatever and bitter, perhaps. I lost the intuition in that period that seemed things were happening from the divine. Like magic, and I have lost the ambition/drive to do like I had before during that period. If Solo Bello came to me now, I wouldn't do it because I have become whatever, passive, and just what is the point? I don't even have the drive/ambition to write, and there are so many stories I want to tell. Waheguru!

Babaji, God & Papa, we aren't promised tomorrow, and it's important not to be afraid. To just do it, and I wasn't going to go to the Beach Bum Tanning on the Bell Blud. In my head, I was saying forget it, but then I saw the pic of Papa & me on my phone. Then I went, and there was nothing to it. I drove there; I know the route and roads through Little Neck, Union Turnpike, & Bell Blud. Pass the condos and Horace Harding.

The streets I grew up on. When I got there, I found parking and had no problems being topless while she sprayed me. Tomorrow, I am flying solo for the 1st time to Sacramento. I realized how I held myself back. Papa must be glad that I am putting myself out there, not scared and not afraid. Papa saw how afraid I was to put myself out there & how held back I was. I think of when Papa told me to find someone on my own. This is for you, Papa. Waheguru!

8/23/21

Babaji, God & Papa, I forgot what sleeplessness in Seattle was about even after watching it so many times as a kid. Watching it on the plane and relating it to her being obsessed with a guy she never met. Seeing signs & asking her friend if she was crazy. Babaji, God & Papa ended up with the guy at the end. My intuition is strong, my intuition isn't wrong, and now the thought of Daniel knowing he saw me that day in the city while on his citi-bike and at Brentt Park during the holidays while holding a plate of pegogis are in my head. I haven't lost my wonder and my beliefs.

I believe. Waheguru!

8/24/21

Babaji, God & Papa, I was packing. I went through Papa's stuff in the basement: the invoices, business cards, and documents. It fills me with such nostalgia. I think of being a witness to how hard Papa worked—seeing him come from a trip and come home to get his briefcase to leave for the office. Him on the phone with clients asking how many bracelets or when Papa was doing 99¢ & asking how many bags. Papa didn't think any job was big or small. Papa did the labor and a physical job. Babaji, God & Papa, I want to write Papa's story. I want the world to know of Papa and the story/experiences of our family. Even Daniel is a story to share since where did that end up? Babaji, God & Papa, I want to tell the stories more than anything & be recognized. I want to leave this Earth, world, & planet, knowing I have left the stories for all people. That would make me very happy. Waheguru!

8/25/21

Babaji, God & Papa, we continued packing today. I took clothes out of Papa's closet, and some of them still had tags. Ma was beside me telling me how she liked buying Papa nice clothes from Bloomingdales & Brooks Brothers. She also puts $100 bills in the pockets of Papa's jacket so his pockets are never empty. Ma is such a devoted wife who nurtured & gave Papa a lot of love & care, even after & now. Ma doesn't want Papa to feel less. That is love, service, & devotion. Ma had shared that now she would push Papa when he wished to eat something or want something.

Ma would say to Papa that he should do it then if he wants it. When we went to grab the totes we had had when we moved from the condo to the triplex, triplex to hear, there were already two totes that said, "Papa's clothes." It was like Papa saying, "Don't forget my clothes."

124

I spent hours with Ma picking out, trying on, and standing in line to pay. Rav said life is about moving on, even though one of your people is not moving on with you. We were talking in the car in front of Whole Foods. I just felt as if I was packing Papa's stuff that he was with us. Papa is moving with us to Rav's house. I took in the scent of Papa from his clothes and his brush. Papa is with us, and this family isn't broken or empty.

Also, I said to Rav that I believe God doesn't do to you something you can't handle. Even though here I was, packing for the third time with my family and the first time without Papa, it didn't feel that way. We did what he would have done if he was here, which was to pack Papa's clothes & stuff. The dream lives on, and we fulfill Papa's dream of moving out of this rental. Rav said that Papa's legacy and his dreams live on from his loved ones, fulfilling them from us fulfilling them since we know them so well. Babaji, God & Papa, I love my tribe, my family, and my people. Waheguru!

8/29/21

Babaji, God & Papa, I think back to what Rav said, "We saw Papa break a lot of phones growing up." I remember sitting in the condo, sitting in the dining area & doing HW. Papa came from the city from work and went straight to the phone to check the voicemail messages. Papa pressed the play button & it was someone who said, "Pal, call me." Papa said, "I went to your office, & you weren't there," in frustration. Then, the next message, and it was the same person who said, "Pal, call me."

Papa pressed the stop button & said, "Panchot," on the phone & threw it. I am sitting calmly. I remember waiting with Papa on the driveway for Ma at the condo. The ice cream truck came by, and Papa got me ice cream. It was the weekend, & Papa was wearing business attire. A button-down plaid shirt and pants with a belt. Papa was very into dressing professionally. It wasn't until I got older that

Papa incorporated polo shirts & jeans. Papa wanted to look professional, smart, & sophisticated. For my sisters and I, it didn't matter what Papa wore because we knew Papa was all these things. However, Papa was very conscious about how he presented himself out there. It mattered to Papa because he was an immigrant, a Sikh-turban-wearing man, and a father/husband. Papa knew he was representing all those groups, and he wanted to be taken seriously. Waheguru!

Morris emailed me that I am teaching 6th-grade science, and I question if she is trying to make my job hard, but jobs should be hard. Papa felt there was no easy job and you should work hard.

Science is new, and I have to make new lesson plans, but I can do it. I can teach any subject, and I have. Babaji, God & Papa, I can't live in fear, and I don't think I am anymore. I got on a plane by myself and went to Sacramento. I never thought I would be able to do that. Babaji, God & Papa, I am making progress and have made progress. I can't compare.

No one is perfect, and no one's life is perfect. Babaji, God & Papa, I don't want to hurt myself by focusing on what might hurt me. I want to do things that will better me and allow me to not live in fear or be scared. I don't want to take action due to fear. I want to be positive, trust my dreams, and put myself out there. I want to love myself and love everything about life. There is nothing to fear. Babaji, God & Papa, I trust you, and you have given me everything I have, and I am grateful for what I have and what you will continue to give me. Waheguru!

After what seemed like the world went upside down and the world I knew changed, finally meeting you and you coming into my life makes me think of two words… AT LAST.

Waheguru!

Think of all the good things that happened today, Harleen. Morris emailed that the NYSESLA scores are out and asked if I want to look at them to use for my tenure binder. Morris is helping me, and that is kind of her. She doesn't have to do that. May, a friend from elementary school, wants to meet up for dinner. Rav is closing on Friday and moving to her new home.

We are getting new furniture after 10+ years. I am getting a queen bed and no more of this twin bed that I have had for 15 years. Anil said you are grown. Jordan is getting the last sport in a Lutheran school in Plainview. Ma is getting her new expensive suits from Zimpy. Babaji, God & Papa, I have to focus on the good things that happened and are happening in my life. Waheguru!

9/27/21

Babaji, God & Papa, are there signs? Does destiny and signs truly exist? Let me write about yesterday when I went to Hicksville LIRR and took the train to Penn. Did it all on my own. As the train took me there I was listening to "Mere satguru tusi menar karo" and thinking of Daniel. I was in total peace. As I walked 34th street, I passed Carmines & thought of his Insta.

Manhattan felt nice & wonderful yesterday. Babaji, God & Papa, I would like to live in Manhattan with my boyfriend, fiancée, husband, companion, and, if space, children. Waheguru!

Babaji, God & Papa, I want my companion, my supporter, my partner, my love, my boyfriend, my lover, my fiancée, my husband & the father of my children. I want Daniel. Waheguru! '

Babaji, God & Papa, thank you for today and the support of Kovacs with the observation with Morris. Kovacs cleaned and helped me, we rehearsed, and the other teachers were nice and supportive by saying good luck & joking. Yesterday, our room won the room contest & 601 got candy & Kovacs & I DD gift cards. The support is not random, and I feel it is the means to make me feel better & part of 167. Morris gave me the option to choose the day, period & class between today and Monday. Also, last year, she gave me the option because she apologized when she didn't come due to the student who committed suicide. I wonder if this choice given to me has to do with the loss. Papa, I don't want that.

Some special treatment because I lost you, Papa. Papa, should I ask Morris why you were letting me choose the class? If there was no personal tragedy, then what? Babaji, God & Papa, tomorrow is my birthday. First, without Papa in the physical sense. Papa would always take me out for dinner. I cherish those memories. It's like a time capsule now, in the past and another world ago. Papa's presence really shaped my world when he was here with us. Now, with Papa not here, it is a different world.

Going through the grieving process, I don't feel like crying now. Babaji, God & Papa, this is life. The way it was to be. Papa would want me to be happy, have fun, accomplish things and not settle due to fear. Papa is with me, with us and Papa was with me today in that classroom when I was getting observed. Papa must be like Harleen you show them, show Morris and everyone. I didn't take you to Court Street in Brooklyn, so you can give up and leave. Rav got her house and new car, and I know it's because where Papa is allows Papa to still do for us. He is still doing his job as a father. Papa is still our father where he is. Waheguru!

Babaji, God & Papa, yesterday Rav, Ma, Jordan & Cole took me to the Plaza Hotel for high tea in the Palm Court. Babaji, God & Papa, there was a wedding going on, and I wonder if it is a sign. I know I will get married and have a wedding if I choose to. I know my career will grow, and my dreams of writing my stories to be in the public arena will happen. Rav then took Mata, and two men were writing "Just Married" on a car.

Then, in the middle of the night, I awoke and felt Daniel's energy. I thought about him and us all night. Then, in my dream, the name "Andrew" appeared. Something like "Andrew is waiting." Babaji, God & Papa, I definitely saw the name Andy in my dream. Waheguru! Waheguru! Daniel's uncle's name was Andy, who passed from my snoop & research. I pulled Papa's picture and asked Papa what this meant & what was going to happen. Waheguru!

Babaji, God & Papa, LHS167, I am just thinking of how a place that was toxic & uninviting became warm & welcoming for me. My birthday was in 2020, when more than half the staff and students were remote. I had that mark on my forehead. It was a Friday, and there was the S.S. remote meeting; Kanowitz was at home and, at the end, she wished me happy birthday. Kanowitz, Rosenberg & Jensen were like it's your birthday. Then I was teaching the five students, and Kanowitz came. He first said, "Happy Birthday," and if Jensen talks back, you talk back. I said I would do that next time. Then the kids wished me. Rosenberg texted me, "Happy b-day," girl. It was thoughtful/nice.

Then December came & after Papa passed, there was an S.S. meeting & Kanowitz &Fekete gave their condolences. I popped my camera on for the first staff meeting, and Vince& Kanowitz were smiling with saying, "Hey."

When we went back into the building in February, Ben stood in front of my door while teaching and waved "Hi" with a huge smile on his face. Wangcame by when I was sitting with Rosenberg and making jokes. Chan was genuinely kind when he came to teach Math to the 6th-grade ELL class.

Chan called the parents when I emailed the teachers/dean about the behavior of the 6th-grade ELL class. I said "Thank you" to him in the hallway. Hall even came to me. Fiona helped in the library with the ICT class to make sure they behaved for my observation. Morris didn't write me up when I didn't call in about Rebecca missing the scantron for the state test. Even this new school year, Kanowitz asked if I met someone in Vegas.

Ben introduced me to his 8th-grade class when I had to give an exit letter to a student, and the class applauded. Kanowitz, Hall and Rosenberg wished me a "happy b-day," with Rosenberg adding it was a beautiful dress. Even Wangwished me after I said congrats to him on his wedding on the 16th. Diaz told me about the Amplify science material and sent it to the room (318).

Kovacs helped me with the informal observation. I saw Brent in the summer at Bleeker, and she has been very nice since she was remote last year. I asked her how the family was. Babaji, God & Papa, it's true that you will find kindness in the places you least expect. Waheguru! I least expected it because of all that happened before, and especially in January of 2019.

Even today when Mayrose asked me to sit next to her on the front steps of the school. Then Mayrose came, and we talked. Babaji, God & Papa, it is the redemption & turning of who did me wrong. Babaji, God & Papa, you always give me the redemption. 701 Advisory. I am okay with staying at LHS167 because I got the justice, clearing & redemption.

Babaji, God & Papa, was it success or successful? Papa had a family that loved him and took care of him in every way, and Ma, Sim, Rav, and I stood by Papa in his struggles, financial and, ultimately, health. Not many people can say that or feel that. Papa was lucky; he had his girls/daughters live with him for a long time, longer than most others, but there was a reason for that. It was for Papa. In my view, Babaji & God do have a bigger dream for you than you can ever dream. Papa is evidence of that. Papa came from parents and siblings who didn't love him. Also thought he wasn't successful or amounted to anything. Yet, Papa got Ma who gave him the social life he never imagined and dressed him like he was royalty. Papa had daughters who saw him the same. You don't take your car or name with you. You take the love, and Papa has a whole lot of that. Babaji, God, Papa, I want to write Papa's story. Waheguru!

Babaji, God & Papa finally had my post-obs with Morris. It was good, and this morning, I woke myself up. I was scared and thinking negatively. I felt she was going to say it was bad and look for work elsewhere. Papa, I cried at home because I would have told you what she said, and you would ask me, "How did it go with the principal?" Babaji, God & Papa, I think of Sept 2020 and coming into 167 with more than half of the staff & kids remote. The Head of Custodian had said this is the place to be. This is paradise. That was in Feb when we went back after 3 months of being remote. In a way, it was Paradise to be at work compared to home, where there were memories. There was support, and people reached out. The job had no pressure, and you were there for the kids to help them learn. Being remote, you have to really connect with people. Waheguru!

Babaji, God & Papa, on Sunday night, as I was lying in bed, I looked at Daniel's picture and said Waheguru three times. Right at that moment, a guy named Evan messaged me on OKC. I liked the conversation between Babaji, God & Papa. He wrote about his instinct that we can be strong. He wrote he wanted to take me to a beautiful beach resort for our first vacation as a couple. Then came all the sweet words of looking at the stars while he had his arm around me and we were drinking red wine. I wrote I'm not too fond of red wine. He said I will make you red pasta, and if I like that. I wrote I do. He asked what wine I liked. I wrote Riesling, and he wrote "Nice" and that I am funny. He wrote we were watching a movie, and he kissed my forehead. I asked what movie. He wrote 50 Dates or Sleepless in Seattle. I wrote I luv Sleepless in Seattle and watched it on the plane from my summer vacation and didn't ask where I went.

He wrote "Nice" and proceeded to write that after dinner, we walked to our suite. I am standing on the balcony looking at waves, and he comes towards me.

He puts his arm around my belly and kisses my shoulder and neck. He pulled me close, and he wrote, "No Gap." That is when the convo turned & it became inappropriate. I wrote I was done with this convo & unmatched him. How could something go from good to bad? Babaji, God & Papa I liked the good parts of the convo.

His describing the beautiful beach resort and being romantic made my day. How did he know that's what I want or one of the things I want? Go on vacation with my boyfriend, my love & my companion/soulmate, Babaji, God & Papa. That convo gave me the same vibes & energy as the like/emoji exchange with Daniel. My mind went to believing it was him. Babaji, God & Papa, it can't be such a coincidence or so ironic that he said he was a general surgeon.

He first wrote, "Please keep smiling." Then, on Saturday morning at 10:30, when I was looking at your picture, wanting him to respond to my "How are you?" and at that moment, he did. I thanked you, Babaji. He mentioned Sleepless in Seattle when I just thought about that when I went to the city for the first facial. The convo was giving me all those vibes and goosebumps. It was a nice convo and I shared it with Rav when we went to the blaze on Saturday night. Rav was like he wasn't responding right away, which shows he isn't looking at the app always & working. But there were mismatches with the pics & Rav said this doesn't seem to be a real person. Hi there, Rodeo wrote Harleen a few times. Hey Harleen, how was grocery shopping? He said he has a sister. Sister is a pediatric resident in Boston and lives in Soho; his ex-girlfriend moved to London & didn't want LDR (Long Distance Relationship) & no ill feelings; he likes concerts, long drives, travel, restaurants, golf, and tennis. I told him I luv tennis and haven't been to courts since the pandemic. I wrote it sounds like a lovely trip.

He asked how grocery shopping was, and I wrote grocery shopping was great. His energy gave me this hype of being direct, witty, and carefree. To be open to writing anything. He wrote teachers are nation builders, didn't ask what I teach, and wrote much respect (for teachers). He said he would grill food on the beach for me. He responds/writes after wishing/praying/saying Waheguru. Asked why are you single? Asked where are you from? Wrote grew up in Queens. Didn't ask if I was Indian. Asked if I have racial preferences. Asked if I lived with family or alone? Said he was born in Tinbeca & grew up there. Babaji, God & Papa, the convo was good, and I was excited until it went the other direction. I second-thought about unmatching, but I didn't want to engage in a convo like that. I want those things. I am a woman, and I am open/want that.

I am not a child or baby. It was the second time chatting, so give me your number, Babaji, God & Papa, I leave it to you, for you know my thoughts, my dreams, and my wants. I have expressed to you, manifested, and prayed. Waheguru!

You have put me on this path to be a strong individual. I am and have put myself out there. I am and have done the work, Babaji, God & Papa. When I started the work, I didn't know I would lose the man/male presence in my life. Babaji, God & Papa, I am strong, and I am ready to be the strong individual of being out there. To be open, ready, awakened, and embrace all you have written for me, Babaji, God & Papa. I am ready, and I am not scared, for what you have in store for me, Babaji, God & Papa. Waheguru! This is my journey (Morris's speech), and I know you have a big, beautiful journey for me, bigger than I can imagine.

11/6/21

Halloween at 167 was nice. Morris stood next to be in the staff picture. Babaji, God & Papa, I didn't know if it was intentional because when I got there, Morris was standing in the middle. She saw me walking to the side and said, "I am going to stand there." She came over. Santiago took a picture of me and Kylie.

I told him perfect time to take a picture. Dylan took a pic of me and Claire. Albert was the one who saw me in the hallway and said to go down because they were taking a staff picture. I am seeing how some of the staff are human. Thank you for that, Babaji, God & Papa. I feel part of a staff/family and I feel like a teacher. I have opened up and become more social. I am not afraid, scared, or in fear.

I am awakened. Morris's actions haven't been unnoticed by me. Her gestures and acts of kindness. (Thanking me for taking Jenny's stuff from her room; I think she picked it up herself) I appreciate Mrs. Morris standing by me. Rosenberg and Yury. Yury told me how Rosenberg has seen her, from being young & single to getting married with kids. Rosenberg said in her career, she has seen all these teachers get married & have kids. She answered me that she would see that happen for me. That was nice for them to say that. Chan came by the library after the Rebecca Scontron situation, but

134

he stood there for a minute & saw me teaching, so he turned around & left. I don't know if he was checking on me to see if I was okay. The people are good, as Wiezbiki once said. I appreciate it all. Waheguru!

11/13/21

Manifestations:

I want to move forward and go beyond horizons I know or am unfamiliar with, always. I don't want to be afraid or scared. I want to be awakened. I want my soul to sail in the direction of my mothership so my life can have meaning & purpose always. I want to live an authentic life that aligns/suits me. I always want to be brave to put myself out there. Papa, you would always say, "Don't be scared; you show them," and "Be strong." I want to broaden my horizons and live around not with what I grew up around. I want different. I want new. I don't want to be an extension of anyone or my life to be one.

I want to grow in my career and get tenure. Papa, you have been and are on this goal with me. My go-to person who gave me advice, pep talks, and cared about my work. So much to always ask, "How is it going?" I want to stay in LHS167. My first day falls on your birthday, Papa. I want to go back and live in Queens or Manhattan. Queens has the roots, and Papa, you love Manhattan. I want to live there with my soulmate and companion. I want to continue teaching kids English. I want to travel. I want to write my stories and the world to hear/read them. Papa, you once said that I would be in Hollywood.

I want my companion and soulmate to be not Indian but American. Papa, you once told me to find him on my own and that you are okay with that. I want him to be supportive, caring, understanding, respectful, loving, and kind/humble. I will be the same to him.

I want him to be intelligent, hard-working, diligent, and open-minded. I want to have my babies, and I want us to be around culture. I would also like to adopt and teach kids around the world who don't have access. Papa, you once said perhaps I will live a life where I won't have to drive a car or have to know. I want to honor Papa and make him proud by writing our family stories and putting them out there. I want to honor my sisters and Ma by writing books and screenplays of our stories. I want to be healthy in mind, body, and spirit. I never want to forget where I come from and the stories. I want the world Ma showed me growing up with her circle/friends to be in the past/closed chapter that I can reference as part of my roots but not part of my current reality or my present and future chapters. Papa, you once said life is chapters. "One chapter closes, and now another new one comes." You said that when Lucky passed away. I want to create a new world for myself different from what I know, used to or seen. I want the stories of my family and me to be on the world stage!

Papa, Ma, and my sisters saw a life bigger, better, and different for me than I could imagine at every step. "So what, you didn't go to the Little Italy festival? Maybe next year you will go to Italy." Papa once said that and so many times when I was disappointed that I wanted to be upset. Papa would be the voice of reason and say there is a reason because something better is coming. Not just Papa but Ma, Rav, & Sim would always give me better than what I settled for.

I was okay with not doing the sweet sixteen because I knew money was tight. Yet Papa, Sim, and Rav made to change that for me, and they gave me more than what I imagined for my 16th birthday. That's what I am trying to say that, at the moment, when someone is giving bigger or more than you could have imagined is meaningful compared to waiting for that bigger or better. However, only family does that, people who care and have an interest in every movement/action in your life. People who care about your happiness and well-being. For me, that is Papa, Ma, Sim, & Rav.

Papa, God & Babaji have many emotions & feelings today. Yesterday was Papa's Varina at Plainview Gurudwara. Seeing Papa's friends since that time after the funeral, when I cried, just brought back emotions. Papa, I miss you. You would be talking to your friends and eating, and I miss your voice, Papa. It's all fresh, vivid, & real for me.

Your presence and your energy I feel, Papa. Sim said, "We are all energy," and that is true. We connect to energies and perhaps some energies we already know or are familiar with. Papa, God & Babaji, that is how I feel about Daniel. All I have is my intuition; my relationship with that put this belief and assurance in me. Papa, bringing him into life in the physical sense, has his energy already entered. Waheguru! Papa, I know you are with us because I know there is an extension to this universe we know that is beyond us and bigger than us. He is in control, and you are there, Papa, watching us & caring for us. Waheguru!

11/28/21

Papa, Raveena is right; I need to be stronger. With everything we have been through as a family. Rav said she didn't give up on the house. She signed one contract & it didn't go through. Rav kept going, and that is how I should be with dating & meeting my one. Never give up. Sim was right that no one is perfect, and it's okay. Sim said if you are giving your time to someone and they aren't giving theirs in return, then you shouldn't do that.

Rav & Sim said to me that if anything, we all should know that time is precious and tomorrow isn't guaranteed. I shouldn't waste time thinking about people who don't think/care about me because I am going to regret that I wasted time/energy. Sim said who is meant to be in your life will be. It will just happen and fall into place. I don't have to chase or do all the work.

Today is Lucky's day, and I know so well where I come from. There is nothing to be ashamed of. Papa, you always knew and would say to me, "You have your sisters." Papa, that is true. Today felt like so many times when I had the heart-to-heart, say it, and everything out with my sisters.

Thank you, Papa. Waheguru! I am not scared, and I shouldn't worry. Papa, God & Babaji are going to give me exactly what I need and even more. Papa is an example of that. You can imagine & hope this much for yourselves, but God & universe gives you more than you could have imagined or hoped for. Papa's parents & siblings didn't expect much from Papa.

However, God & universe did so he brought Mom into Papa's life. Papa's life completely changed for the better. Papa is getting all dressed up to go to their fancy parties. I don't think my grandparents could have imagined that or Papa's daughters becoming lawyers. That's God & the universe. Waheguru!

I am grateful
- For my career at LHS167
- For my family
- For my ability to write.
- For never having to do grades while teaching summer in DoE
- For things always falling into place
- For meeting kind people
- For my students
- For the love I have in my life
- For the people I work with, who I have learned from, who are kind, share their stories, and work hard.
- For God always finding a path and an opportunity for me
- For not being perfect
- For my carpool buddy Anna Markis
- For the ability to see situations as okay when it starts as not being okay
- For having faith and believing it will be okay even if it feels not that way
- For being able to make peace & find peace
- For right now, nothing feels okay, but believing that it will all be okay and feel okay.
- For Claire Kovacs, who is being a great co-teacher and supporting/helping me with 601 & my observations
- For Mrs. Morris supporting me and bringing Debbie Winkler to the school to help me
- For Stella Katsoras & her humor support
- For him, Blake's support and printing my worksheets from her home
- For John Fekete's push to speak at the Margaretann Cuchiarra training and him telling me what to do.
- For a vehicle to get me places
- For my strength
- For "Beautiful Me training."

Yesterday, I had coverage in the room that I was in/I used my first two years in Heinter's room, where I had two observations, pull-out kids and the homerooms. I can say I am not that nervous person anymore. 5 years ago seems like so long ago. I had coverage in there last year & Katsoras stopped by to bring lunch. I wonder if it was an excuse to check on me. It's all good, God, Babaji. It's okay, Papa.

Papa, God & Babaji, what is intuition? For me, it's the messages and signs God gives me. Messages in my dreams and the signs I see. Papa, my dreams are my messages from God & Babaji. The signs I encounter as I live my life are messages from God & Babaji. So my intuition is correct and valid, Papa.

What I believe is correct; otherwise, why would God & Babaji put those messages in my dreams and show me those signs in my everyday routine? Papa, God & Babaji wouldn't have me dream those dreams or see those signs to trick me or play with my emotions. Papa, God has given me the answers and revealed some truth. Allowed me to connect the dots. Papa, you know, can you let me know? Waheguru!

An IG account of Dr. Mark requested to follow me. Who is this truly? Last night, a Sukh account. Who is behind them? I want to know. Last night, an account named "Sukh" requested to follow me & then went. Who are all these accounts truly? Who is it?

Papa, you gave us signs and messages. You didn't worry, Papa, because of your faith and the peace you made with so many things. Also, you knew that Ma, Sim, Rav, Jordan, Cole, & I would be okay. We would be okay because we have each other and are strong. I feel the fact that my first day at LHS 167 falls on your birthday, Papa, is a sign. The times I tried to find a job elsewhere and the interviews/demos I got. Yet, here I am, and it's a sign that this is the school I am meant to teach in. The universe aligned those important dates together and presented them to me as a sign. Waheguru! I think of Gabby, the custodian said last school year with the remote option. He said this is the place to be. This is paradise. JHS 167 truly was when we went back in February 2020, 1 month after Papa passed away. I felt support and worked the medicine to turn to.

12/15/21

I am awakened, Papa, Babaji & God. This morning, as I drove to work with Angela, I felt the need to tell her what I did. I wanted another perspective. So I told her hypothetically, thinking of Nancy's daughter. I messaged her and realized she is the age of Daniel & the gf. I feel Angela's direct and aggressive tone was the wake-up. She was appalled by the cousin's actions which are mine. Her words, "She never spoke to him, so why is she bothering him." "He has a girlfriend." "He is living his life; he has a right to. Why is she stalking him." "It's sad. She was finding comfort in something that wasn't there." "She was just infatuated and spending all her time on this." "That's dangerous." Papa, Babaji & God, I realized how wrong & immature I behaved. Angela was upset at how this girl was behaving, like over a guy.

I am sorry, Papa, Babaji & God.

12/17/21

Papa, you would love the home Raveena bought. I can imagine you walking in the home. Plainview Gurdwara is nearby. Papa, can you give me an image in my dreams of my companion & partner? Papa, give me an image of my future and lie. This morning, I had a dream. Sim said, "I can see that in 9 years, you will be." I woke up and said, "Famous." Papa, I am grateful. Today, I had the "Beautiful me" training. Pap, I spoke and shared. It ended at 11:30 AM, and the other teachers, Kelly & Laura, said, "hide." I drove to get my nails done. Papa, Babaji & God, I appreciate the day I had. It was nice, and I am grateful. Waheguru!

12/18/21

Papa, Babaji & God, I watched the Indian movie Kabhie Khushi Kabhie Gum today. It was an old movie, and Ma, Rav, Sim, and Jordan enjoyed it. I got so into enjoying a movie that I forgot the arm pain from the booster. Papa, you loved watching movies. I realized when you think of the pain, it doesn't go away. When you are genuinely enjoying something, then the pain isn't on your mind. Papa, you want me to enjoy and enjoy genuinely. Papa, you wouldn't want me to be frustrated and drive myself nuts with the dating apps, the guys who aren't serious, and Instagram. Papa, you wouldn't want me to just constantly be on my phone looking at the apps and Instagram. Papa, I just felt that I needed to find someone & have something immediately. I guess to fill the loss or a prize. I guess it goes back to when I was a kid.

Papa, I got better grades in MS & HS than Rav & Sim. Papa, I liked showing you my report cards with 90% & above averages, my articles from my high school newspaper, my articles from the Indian Tribune, and my high test papers. I liked sharing that with you, Papa, because I wanted you to be proud of not just me but of yourself. Look what your child has done.

I remember I interviewed some representatives that Tanvi brought to Plainview Gurdwara. I was in college, and later, Tanvi brought the man to Papa. Tanvi said to the man, "This is the father of the young lady who interviewed you." I was standing not far from Papa, and the man said to Papa, "Your daughter asked great questions and has a bright future." Papa, I remember your expression. You were speechless and felt raised when the man shook your hand. Papa, I know you were proud of us because of our close bond with you. I don't need to bring something to show you quickly. Papa, you want me to be genuinely happy & do the things I enjoy. Waheguru!

1/8/22

Papa, Babaji & God, my first writing in the new year. What is Intuition? For me, intuition is God's messages and God communicating about what to believe. Papa, correct me if I am way off about this. It's my intuition that makes me believe that it was Daniel on the bike that day I went to Central Park Zoo with Jordan, his, and Rav. It's my intuition that makes me believe that it was Daniel standing with glasses & a blue bubble jacket near the stalls at Brentt Park Holiday Market on Christmas. He saw me and Rav with Cole in my LV bag. It's my intuition that makes me believe it was Daniel with his friends at a table near Rav & Sim when I came with Pegagis at Brentt Park Holiday Market in 2019.

He looked at me as I was walking to the table and sitting. It's my intuition that makes me believe Evan& Sean (OKC) are Daniel. Papa, this is what my intuition says, and I feel this is what God is communicating to me to believe. If I am wrong, please let me know, Papa. I was out four days from work because I was not taking care of myself. I will now. Wake up call. Waheguru!

Papa, Babaji & God, I remember in the Triplex, Papa, you came up to me in the kitchen and said, "Find someone on your own, okay." Papa, you said it so sweetly, genuinely, and calmly. Then 2020, and perhaps, I was so adamant about messaging Daniel because I wanted to start something rolling. Papa. I prayed & negotiated with God & Babaji. I said if not for me, then do it for Papa. Bring my person to me so Papa can see my wedding or at least see me with my person. Rav got angry when I told her that. I understand because I never talked to Papa about guys or my wedding or future visions in that regard. Perhaps because I never grew up with those visions or imagining that. Also, Papa had his pride & dignity and didn't even want Bunty to see him weak & sick.

So Papa wouldn't want to see my person in the condition he was in. We never got a timetable in 2020, but the last time Papa went to the hospital, it was obvious. That night, Rav told us the obvious from the hospital. Sim was angry at the world. Ma and I cried in the living room. I said to Ma that I guess Papa was physically present for my wedding, and all wasn't to be.

Ma looked at me and said, "Koi baat nahi." "It's okay," and then Ma said, "45 years with your Papa, I spent." Papa, all I can write is that you not being here is a missing piece and an absence. We have each other, so we will be okay and are okay because we are strong. It's okay because I will share my memories and stories of you, Papa, with all my dear ones now and to come. My person and my kids included. To the world, Papa. They will know how very present and alive you are still to me. Your soul, spirit, and energy, Papa, will never fade because I will keep it eternal & alive in my life. You are my guiding light. Waheguru!

Harleen, you have been through so much and have overcome so many obstacles & barriers, and blocks. Harleen, you have been strong and are strong. Harleen, when Shalu & Mo would just call up some guy to pick them up & go somewhere, I didn't go. Instead I went home and turned around to my way home. It was hard & I took a breath. I did that knowing who I was & my dignity. I didn't need a stranger to go places. You associate with immaturity and people of not your level then you become that. At that time, I didn't want to be that. After Shalu & Mo, I didn't have the bffs or close friends like that, but who cares? That isn't important. It would be a shame, after everything in my life so far, to act immature. Knowing that you don't take anything with you but love that is in your life. Life is not about showing off perfection or moments but about leaving a real legacy and leaving love for the ones dear to you. Waheguru!

2/4/22

The main problem in my father's life was financial. The last seven years for my dad were great. The worries that consumed my dad about how to pay these bills and having enough money were not there. It was all taken care of, and my father was enjoying his life. Simran once said to me that, in the end, everything balances and evens out.

There is an Indian movie line, "In the end, everything is okay." Of course, for us, as a family, we didn't know those were the last years of my father. Jordan's Lohri patty at 5 months felt like now the good times and memories are here. After my father's passing, it was hard.

I didn't get the tenure and got my second extension. I didn't get a boyfriend to show off as "look what I got." Continue working hard. It was the universe saying I was not done yet. It's not the end for me. That was hard for me to understand.

I remember after my father's passing, a senior teacher at work, the speech teacher asked me how I was doing. I said it's hard. She said you must know that was your father's journey, and you have your journey. I said I guess, but it's hard when you always see it as connected. I understand how feeling we are on the same journey happened. As a family, we were a team with the same goals of making sure there was structure, everything was being paid, and we were helping each other with our problems. I get solace remembering something my father said when our first family dog, Vicki, passed away. This is one chapter. There will be other chapters.

Babaji, God & Papa, I am grateful that at work, I am around people who are good & telling me their flaws in teachings & being honest. Dylan says that if she gets obsessed with 601, it would be ineffective. Costanza came and said she had no control of 791. Cynthia Sable is saying she has no money & is rethinking her choice of being a teacher (she pays $2,600 rent).

Fekete says the bad people are gone (Marilyn & Janet). He even said to Janet that you are evil. Even in the summer, that gym teacher said the first years are always tough/hard. The first few years, I should have talked to people and listened at work so that I wouldn't have been hard on myself that I wasn't good & I shouldn't be here. But who I was around the first years were people who had an ego & wouldn't admit that they found it hard or they struggled. They weren't humble to do that. Rav said the bad crop of people. It's the journey, and it's all right. Morris says "Hi, Ms. Sahni" to me all the time now. She even had the students stop and let me go out first. I guess I got her respect. Now, I need to respect myself and carry confidence. Waheguru!

Ma said to me the other day that I should think of Papa as Babaji & God. I remember the day when I prayed, and I had to stop & edit. Papa went from being part of my prayers to who I prayed to. My prayer opening changed. For me, it was just all of a sudden. One day changes everything suddenly. It reminds you to be grateful because life can change in an instant. Papa, you are my God and my Babaji. I know you are watching, and even when I get upset with all my emotions, I find peace in prayer, God, and with you, Papa. Papa, I know you are listening, and you have kept me strong from breaking and destroying myself completely. Papa, you will bring me the happiest days in my life. Papa, you kept me strong during the worst day of my life. Papa, I have my memories to share with the world, my soulmate, and my children. Waheguru!

Papa, and God & Babaji, the times I got really sad & emotional, I turned to Ma. The Valentine's Day of 2021 & today. Rav is busy with Jordan& work, so she gets frustrated & doesn't have that time anymore. I understand, so Ma is who I turn to, and MA has risen to the occasion. Ma was the last to turn to. For me, it was Rav & Sim & Papa. Sim moved to Cali, so it became Rav. When Rav had Jordan in 2019, it became Papa who gave the words of wisdom & comfort. Today, I got emotional telling Ma that I don't feel I have time and I feel I need to do things quickly. Like a clock, which I told Claire. Ma told me about the guy she liked but didn't marry. She thought it was for the best, & Papa was great. I remember first hearing about this guy in the condo & Rav said the lesson is your parents already shape your kid's destiny. If Ma married someone else, then our lives & where they would have to be would have differed. This guy said to Ma you faired better because she would have been miserable in Kanpur. Ma also said one thing about Papa: he always found a way or a way/solution presented to him to complete a task. Ma said Papa would tell her that a lot. "Raaste nikhil ta hai." I told Ma that Papa was lucky because he had the support of his kids & family. Some families don't have that. Ma said that is true and we were lucky since people have it hard, like Vinderjeet & Gurvir. We always stayed in Bayside for 30 years. I told Ma about what I believe in the end, it's all good & happy. Even though we didn't know it was the last, Papa was happy & he threw that Lohri party for Jordan. Papa knew and saw the future. Sim went back in 2020 & was happy in Cali with Anil. Rav had Jordan & he was the future. Ma was happy with him. Papa saw me in my career. Ma said I go to the temple & I should be positive. Waheguru!

2/26/22

Papa, I was thinking about you last night. My memories went to the times you dropped me. For instance, in Astoria, for the teaching certification test. I remember I told you I would be done in two hours. You said you will come in two hours. I wasn't done in two hours, and I saw your missed calls when I went into the bathroom. I came to be lobby, and I saw you standing there—Papa with a teacher or principal of the school. I knew what happened, you came & didn't see me. I wasn't picking up the calls, and you got worried and went inside. He told everyone & the security guards that I was waiting for my daughter. When you saw me, you laughed & said, "You're done with the test." The man next to you said your dad was worried & I told him that the test isn't timed, so when the person feels they are done. I said "thank you" to the man, and he asked me how the test was. Papa, I remember you came with me for the interview at JHS 167. You inspected the neighborhood and said it's a posh area.

In the summer of 2019, Sim was here, and Ma, Sim, Papa Cole & I went to Atlantic City. Rav just had Jordan, so she stayed home. The road trip to Atlantic City was one you did a million times, Papa. From the age of 5, I remember going with you for your business on the boardwalk. There was a time as a kid I just didn't want to go anymore. It was the same boardwalk, soft-serve ice cream, funnel cake, and saltwater taffy. But I was a kid & couldn't be left home alone.

I remember one time I threw up on your pants, Papa, & you continued driving to AC. Summer of 2019 became our last road trip to AC, and through all the years, one thing remained true up until the end: we liked spending time with each other and enjoyed being around each other. I was in my 30s & Sim was in her 40s; spending weekends with my parents & going to the mall was a fact. It wasn't a trend I saw with others, and perhaps in some aspects, I still felt like a kid. Papa, that is what you gave me, along with so much more.

Thank you, Papa, for all you did for me, including the drop-offs. It's my fault I didn't want to grow up and still wanted to act like a kid. Thank you, Papa, for how you made me feel. Protected and loved. Waheguru. How you made me feel, Papa, is what made you extraordinary and powerful, and it's the best gift you gave me. I hope I can find a way to feel those things on my own. Ma, Rav, & Sim make me feel that way. I hope my companion and partner make me feel that way. I hope the gift of those feelings is always offered to me, Rav, Sim, Ma, Cole, and Jordan. Waheguru!

3/3/22

Papa, my first day as a teacher at JHS 167 falls on the same day as your birthday. That is my answer. I am where I am supposed to be. When you don't know, look towards the universe for the answers, and you will know.

Papa, that is what I am going to think of and believe. I got the email tonight that Morris and Dr. Mark (deputy superintendent) are coming to visit me and Kovacs on Monday morning. Ariel called me in period 1 today and said the ELL office is getting new rolling office chairs. Then Ariel asked how are the chairs. Papa, is this the make me feel good act? Kovacs said she wouldn't come to us if she didn't trust us. So, I feel I am a good teacher, Papa. I will be fine, and more than fine. I will be strong and show them, Papa, as you said to me as our advice to me when I was having a hard time at work. Waheguru!

149

Papa, today I got on the LIRR & went on a date via It's Just Lunch. The guy wasn't a click, but I did something I never did before. That requires praise and is something, Papa, I still believe in magic, love, destiny, soulmates, past-life connections, meant-to-be, love at first, signs, and fate. Papa, thank you because I have come a long way. I walked into STK with confidence and independence. Still knowing where I come from and who I am. Still remember the memories and sharing those with Ma's friends who came over last night for Ma's kitty in the house. Papa, we all felt your presence at the kitty. Ma took a picture with all the uncles & your picture was in the middle. It was like you were there, Papa. Papa, you are with us. I felt you were with me as I was on the train going to the city today. I believe me being confident is the best thing I can do for you, Papa. It's the gift I can give you. You have given me so many gifts, Papa. Waheguru!

Spring Break

Papa, I remember our last summer in 2020. We were sitting on the sofa, and you were praying, Papa. I was sitting next to you on my cell phone. When you finished praying, you closed the holy book and held it between your palms. Then you turned towards me, and you bowed your head towards me. I looked at you but didn't ask why you did that because usually you just bow looking straight. I looked back at my cell phone and just thought that you were giving me your prayers and telling Babaji to bless me.

Papa, now I feel that was your way of telling me that you were leaving. At that moment, you weren't praying for yourself anymore but for your family. Papa, you were telling me you were leaving and that it's okay because you will be with Babaji. Papa, you are in the position to bring good things to Ma, Sim, Rav, Jordan, Cole & I.

I feel, Papa, that when you were here, you saw us accepting situations and making the best of what we had. Papa, I don't know if you were satisfied with that because you were the ultimate girl's dad who did anything for his girls to your ability. That's okay because every parent does the best to their ability. Papa, you are with Babaji. You are in a position to make things happen. You have already when Rav got her home.

Bringing blessings our way from where you are. It doesn't surprise me because I know I have a great father who always did for me and my sisters. Papa, you are still doing for us though you aren't with us in the physical sense. How lucky and blessed I am. God gave me such an extraordinary father. Waheguru!

Papa, I can't waste my energy. The other day, I got myself sick in the stomach and stressed Ma, Rav, & Sim. Papa, over Daniel. I never met him, or did I? Was he the one on the bike and in Brentt Park? Papa, I got one closure and answer.

The person on Instagram who messaged me as Dr. Mark wasn't really Dr. Mark. Papa, I thought, though, but that's the fantasizing part of me. I am not going to react to any of Dr. Mark's stories because he deletes them. So that's done. Papa, Daniel blocked me on Instagram and Facebook. He has gone into the category of Manjot, Manav, their wives, and parents. Also Harmeet. Papa, I blame myself. It's my thinking of creating something and reality being something else.

Don't Go To Speed Dating Event

Papa, the other day, I was looking at my credit report. I remembered in the triplex how we would look at my credit report together. You told me how to dispute something on my credit report. You would tell us that it's important to have a good credit score in this country. You can't get anything without good credit, is what you told us. Papa, we have come a long way. That was so many years ago, and you must be happy because I wasn't checking my credit report for the past few years. My credit score was good. Papa, in my head, I am telling this to Daniel. He tells me to put all of those experiences/memories in a time capsule and live for now so you can put all of it in another time capsule. Papa, why am I having this convo with Daniel in my head? I think of him, and all this insight & perspective comes. This connection I feel comes through when I think of him. Papa. I don't know what to do. I know you are watching Papa. It's all good. Waheguru!

Who I Want

Papa, Babaji, and God, I want someone kind, humble, slightly arrogant, confident, hardworking, and diligent. I want him to be good-looking, tall, and nicely fit. I want him to come from a big family with siblings, cousins, parents, grandparents & nieces/nephews. I want him to be funny like Papa and like good food. I want him to be stylish and dress well. I want a doctor and surgeon who has an excellent education at a good university. I want him to be rich and have his own place in the city. I want him to be social, famous, Jewish and have a lot of friends. I need his connections to produce my stories in Hollywood.

He needs to have connections in Hollywood and Entertainment. I want him to respect me and take care of me so I can publish my stories to an audience. I want him to support my dream and career. I want him to be super romantic, and we are always loving each other. I want to get pregnant and conceive this July. I want him to be the opposite of me. I want us to serve and adopt as well.

I want him to have a grown-up here. I want him to be tall and not Indian. I want him to be my friend, and we talk about everything. Because he is privileged and the privileged life he lives, he finds my upbringing stories fascinating. He finds me stronger than him, and my life experiences are harder than his. I want him to be young, and I am attracted to him to be young, and I am attracted to him physically & emotionally, every day. I want us to have an emotional, spiritual, and past-life connection.

He provides me with emotional support, cares for me and provides for me financially as well. I want him to be a good provider, a daredevil, and a good father. I want him to enjoy learning about other cultures and diverse foods like me. I want him to have family values and be family-oriented like Papa. Papa, bring him to me. Yes, I am ready! Waheguru! I am ready to step into the dream/life you have for me, Papa, Babaji & God.

05/20/20

Papa, Babaji & God, today was the last observation of the school ear. Jenny said, "You got through a hell of a year." I think 2020 was a hell of a year. In the morning, Brent came cheery & swaying to take Maria for the pledge. In the morning announcement Brent quoted Ghandi about "no culture can live if it attempts to be exclusive." Today was culture day. After the observation, I asked Katsoras if she wanted Dunkin & she took my offer. She joked if this would do anything for my observation. I said I expect highly effective, and Rebecca is my witness. Everyone was nice. Fabrizio was talking about his Indian food. I pointed out his Italian jersey, and I said I don't have anything Indian (where my parents are from).

Blake asked about my observation & was genuinely listening & happy. Papa, the observation went well, and I wish I could see your face & tell you. Papa, it's all good at work. Papa, it's all good. Waheguru!

06/4/22

Papa, Babaji & God, with everything that has happened these past two years, I am going back to old ways in a way. I bought one month of Nutrisystem and cheated, feel disappointed that I didn't lose at least 10 pounds. I am going back to feeling not good about myself and angry. Papa, I don't feel hopeful about meeting my one. I feel that I am too old, and it's too late. All the money wasted on charts, tarot and psychics. Papa, I have to change my ways. Despite all this, Papa, you bring people to me who are in the same boat. Claire was on an anti-depressant and gained weight from her break-up. It took her two years to take his pics off her Instagram now.

We were talking about that. About losing someone where the life you knew changes forever. Papa, I have to believe and believe that I am where I am supposed to be. I will have everything I want and not worry. I don't need to be scared because you have a bigger dream for me than I can ever imagine. Waheguru!

6/10/22

Oh, Papa, Babaji, and God, I was told I might be exhausted. Why Papa? I worked so hard. I don't want to look for another school. Work in a bad area. Papa, why is this happening? This isn't fair, and it's discrimination. Papa, help me. This is wrong. Papa, keep me strong. Papa, give me justice. Waheguru! Waheguru! Waheguru!

Papa, Morris told me I am being excessed on Friday. Papa, I thought my first day being on your birthday and you seeing me at 167 meant that I would finish my teaching career for however long at 167. Papa, I know what the plan was that I would trach and pursue the writing. That got side-tracked at 167 because the job is too much work. Papa, I also know what I prayed & wished for. To meet someone that lives in the city but I wanted to make that change when it happens. Papa, Morris doesn't like me, and that is a factor in this. Papa, I have to fight another battle.

Papa, I know if I am not happy at work or where I am, then I can't attract a guy or anything I want. Papa, I want the tenure, and it looks like I have to fight for that. Papa, if I can just get the tenure and have to work at another school so then be it. Papa, I surrender to you, Babaji, and God. Papa, I will fight and stand up all I can. Papa, I leave it to you. What would you have me do, Papa? Papa, I miss you, and I love you always. Waheguru, Waheguru, Waheguru.

Papa, Babaji & God, when I approached Katsoras on Friday. She said, "What belongs to you can't be taken from you." I found that a coincidence because when I wrote how I would feel when I got tenure, part of it was, "What is meant for you and where you are meant to be can't be interrupted." I wrote that believing 167 is where I am meant to be, and the sign was that my first day was Nov. 7th, 2016. Papa, perhaps I am wrong.

My purpose and where I am meant to be is somewhere else, but 167 is the interruption. Papa 167 came into my life when I needed to leave RT and make more money. Sim left for Cali, and Rav was worried if Sim was still going to give $500 for rent, which she did. It was a dire situation, and I had found a job in East Flatbush, but no way Ma would have me work there. So I refused, and what did Babaji and God do, Papa? He brought a sweet gift of 167, which was 15 minutes from home.

So I could take local since I was comfortable with local streets. In the beginning, 167 was great, and I got to work in District 26 in the summer. I really feel Babaji and God found a way to help me, Rav & our family by giving me 167.

I felt lucky that it was close and convenient, and it all fell into place with findingMrs. Sainito ride with on snow days or emergencies since she lives a block away. 167 has served its purpose, and when that is the case, then all that is left is to move on. I couldn't make that decision, so someone else did, and it's not in my control. When Morris told me, I felt a sense of content because it affirmed my belief that God, Babaji is listening to everything I pray for. Focus on writing the stories, meeting someone who lives in the city and starting my own family is now all possible. In 2020, before Papa passed away, the psychic Hitesh said my life purpose is to create or a creative purpose and I need to leave the teaching job. I told her I needed to be financially secure & needed income. So, the decision has been made. Even though every year I looked in the open market & went on demos, it wasn't the right time. It's true that God's time is not our time. Perhaps God saw how just this past year I hated that commute, and even though God, Babaji, helped by finding a carpool person in Markis (again, God's looking out). Yet Babaji and God are saying it's time to move on and do your purpose, Harleen. This job was a need of a circumstance at that time in 2016. Those circumstances are gone.

Yes, I need a job to pay my bills. I proved & impressed myself by learning Spanish & connecting with kids from a different region. But the truth is I was a film studies major, and I remember Ben hearing that said you should keep pursuing that. Yes, with 167, I took two screenwriting classes at the New York Film Academy, but I couldn't pursue it with all the work, visits, and drama that came over the past 2 to 3 years. Papa, I don't need to be scared and anxious about going into 167 next week, which is the last week of school. This is the freedom that Papa, Babaji & God orchestrated. This is the affirmation that I can have all I dreamt of in the past two years. I have changed, and what I want has changed since 2016.

156

Yes, since 2016, I have seen women at work get engaged, married, and have kids. Yes, I wasn't able to have those changes in my personal life, but that goes to what Rav said: if a job is not allowing you to grow in your personal life, then you need to leave that job because you aren't happy. It's Babaji, God & Papa saying you can have all those things, but you need to leave this place. I will not be leaving with nothing, and I have my experience and, hopefully, my tenure. Waheguru! Diego said in a tenure meeting that some people shouldn't be teachers. I don't know if she was referring to me, Brooke, or someone else. I am a teacher and a good teacher who has taught English to ELLS for a long time.

I validate myself. God, Babaji and Papa validates me. Perhaps this is their way of saying that you did your service here. Going back to things Papa said to help me with this. Papa said life is chapters; one chapter closes, and another one opens. I didn't think I would have to use that for this. I thought of that when Sim and I spoke about Papa in the gurdwara. Also, when we moved to Plainview. Now, with the excessing, that is what makes Papa an extraordinary parent. A parent's legacy and Papa's legacy are the words & advice insight he shared with us that still help me with all the unpredictable moments. I think of all that, and I refer to those words (even though Papa isn't here in the physical sense) and that is what keeps Papa present and that you are never really gone but heavily here with us. Waheguru! Papa!

6/26/22

Papa, Babaji & God, tomorrow is the last day of the school year. I have been exhausted, so my last day at 167 unless the #'s go up and I return due to need. Papa, Babaji & God, only you know what's best for me & what's to happen. I would be okay to come back because I have learned & I know what's important to focus on. Creating boundaries & knowing this is a job. I am not worried, Papa. Waheguru!

Papa, yesterday Rav said you came with your own destiny, just like everyone does. Papa, if I get married and have kids, which I want. Papa, I want 5 kids if I can. Papa, for you to not see that for me in the physical state and be near me was the way it was to be. I have to accept that, Papa. It's not just me, but so many people lose a parent at an even younger age. Rav said my life isn't intertwined with yours, Papa. It felt that way because we lived together. Papa, with 167, I was upset because I thought my first day being on your birthday was a sign that it was my place. Papa, are there signs, or do we make them up? Perhaps the sign is that the job was for the family. Perhaps it's time to move on to better and do a job where I can pursue my passion for writing.

Perhaps, end the chapter asyou believe, Papa. Perhaps I need to leave 167 to move on & heal because of the memories of Glen Oaks & Papa dropping me at times. Papa, I don't know, and only time will tell why. I wouldn't have decided to leave 167, so the decision was made for me. Papa, I am not the only one and others got excessed. Kovacs packed up her stuff, too, & her dad came to pick up her stuff. Papa, I think I know what I did with Daniel. I made his IG a T.V. show that I tuned into, like Saved By The Bell. It goes back to what I did as a kid. Wanting to be part of something, so imagining myself there. For example, Growing Pains Full House, Empire, and Buffy. Papa, that's my mind. Papa, you were sick, and I was imagining my life with Daniel.

The one I wanted, and I feel I took you for granted, Papa. Perhaps that is why I kept saying 'sorry' at your funeral. I remember in 2012, I got into an accident & you came when I was in the ambulance. You were worried & asked "if I was okay." I said, "Yeah, Papa." Papa, you know I am emotional. Papa, I don't want to forget the rotis I made because Ma was in India. I was in H.S. Papa.

I don't want to forget the condo, Triplex, & Glen Oaks. I want to remember all the moments and memories, Papa. Waheguru! Papa, I just want to be happy. Papa, you are with Babaji and at a place where you foresee everything for Ma, Sim, Rav, Jordan, Cole, and me. You are making things happen like Rav getting the house Plainview. Papa, you assured me that when you did mata towards me on the sofa that summer. Papa, that mata is powerful, and it's why you wouldn't want me to worry.

It's powerful knowing you are with Babaji and can make things happen, but also foresee then reassure us, Papa. Perhaps that is why I need to leave 167 so I can be happy. Papa, you want me to be happy and not accept situations like we had to before because of the financial problems. Not settle with a job because you don't know better and because we needed the money. As Brooke said, this is not a bad thing. Waheguru! Papa, whenever I see an IG story of Daniel, he seems perfect. He knows how to cook, smart, then why Papa isn't he with me? There is a reason, and there are other perfect guys out there. He isn't the only one, Papa. And who is he, Papa? I never met or spoke to Daniel.

It's a T.V. show, Papa. It's not real. Everything you see is not everything. It's an image that has been preconceived. Papa, I would want my boyfriend to be friends with my siblings, mom, and older family members on Facebook. That's not the case there, even though it's not my place to judge. Papa, I don't want to be jealous. Papa, I can't stop my mind being fixated. Papa, I don't know what to do about this. Waheguru! Waheguru! Waheguru! Let it be!

Papa, I am sorry, but I don't want to live anymore. Please bring me to you. I am not positive anymore about anything. I am a mess that is not getting any better. Papa, I want to be with someone. I want to experience love. I want to be pregnant, have kids & start a family. I want to write our stories and want them to be published and on the screen for an audience. I want Jordan to talk. I want the tenure, and I thought I would stay at 167, but I did not … so well. I don't want to put any energy into looking for another job. I don't care, Papa. I am tired, and now, Papa, you have to show me. Papa, bring all I want to me now. Papa, I am tired of waiting. I can't wait anymore. I am tired of this life. I become the crazy one over and over. Papa, I have become a fool many times, and I feel like nothing. There is nothing, no destiny, fate, signs, and hope. I am done, Papa. Waheguru! Papa, there is a lesson Babaji, God, and the universe want me to learn. I am not learning it, and that is why I ended up in the ER in January and yesterday in the city. I have to take care of myself before I can meet anyone. Need serious goals & have to follow through with them.

1. Lose weight.

2. Finish the tenure website.

3. Finish screenplay.

4. Put myself out there.

5. Do things I enjoy and have fun.

6. Meet people.

7. Have faith in Babaji, God & Papa are watching& doing for us.

8. Spend more time with Jordan

9. Be there for Ma, Rav & Cole.

10. Be positive.

Waheguru! Waheguru! Waheguru!

I want to be with my life companion.

I want to finish my screenplays.

I want to have my babies (5 babies) kids.

I want the tenure & stay at 167 if I can.

I want to lose weight and be healthy.

Papa, I was looking at your picture the other night, and a feeling came over me. The picture felt real, like it came to life, and I looked at your eyes. I felt you were truly looking at me, and I know, Papa, you are watching all of us. Papa, you know what belongs to us. Please give us a peek. Waheguru. Papa, I had a dream that I was wearing a green dress and walking to a stage to accept an award. In the past, I have imagined a green dress that is rooted in a Banana Republic shirt I brought.

It had embroidery on the collarbone. I imagined a dress & going to the Oscars. I know my purpose. Papa, the prayers and mata did produce something. Hope & belief. Perhaps the excessing has its purpose/reason. Darji, Bhari Mami, Nanaji, & Nani and Papa. They are not here. I feel this immense responsibility to tell their stories. I want people to understand the environment I was in with all of them. What was it like being around them, and what were they like? I want to honor them.

Papa, so much is going through my head. There is so much I want. Being with my companion, getting my stories & screenplays out there, losing weight, Jordan talking, getting tenure, and being in a school for September if that is to be. Papa, I am surrendering all these wants to you and Babaji. I don't know what to do to get most of those things. I know I have to stick & follow through with a diet. I have to sit and finish the screenplay. I sat and worked on the tenure website. I am applying for jobs on the open market. I have joined Meetup Script Camp online groups. I try to help Jordan with talking. Papa, with the companion part.

I am on Hinge App, but I think of Daniel, Papa. I still daydream and hope. Papa, I say I love him. I can't let go, Papa. Perhaps it is important to do what you love; otherwise, the plate will be full of wants/things. Waheguru! I can write forever, Papa. The teaching is not love, perhaps, and that is why love didn't come my way, or I couldn't find my love.

7/15/22

Papa, Babaji & God, I can't freeze my eggs now because it's too expensive, and my insurance doesn't cover it. Papa, I know you already informed me not not to worry, Papa. I want three kids. Two boys and a girl. I have their names: Gajinderpal (Pal), Andy, & Meher. Papa, after you passed, Mehar appeared in my dream. I believe all my dreams during that time, even the ones with Daniel, were my sixth sense & intuition. Telling me what's to come and what is to be.

I believe that Papa. This is just the waiting period. Papa, I don't know if getting excessed from 167 is you & the universe saying stop the teaching & do your stories/screenplays. I know all the things I expressed to God & things I wrote, like feeling trapped/forced. Papa, is this your "You are free & released cuz there is no situation anymore." I know God listens, and Papa, you are with Babaji, so double the ears. I need to write everything that happened in the past two years before I forget the feelings of those events.

Papa, I need to finish that screenplay. Papa, you are with me. Waheguru! Papa, why was my first day at 167 on your birthday? What is the reason for that? What will happen with the tenure, Papa? Waheguru! Perhaps those 15-year-old feelings, reactions, and mindsets in the past two years need to change/go for the waiting period to end.

That is what Sim said. You were acting like a teenager, & I don't believe that it's my fault because I didn't have the experience dating, talking to guys, & how to know if they are interested. Papa, it's okay. Waheguru! I am only on Hinge. I am embracing my life as it is. Just being and not obsessing or fixated on anything. Just calm and quiet. I love my waiting, Papa. Going to my roots as how I was and how I am. Papa, it's okay. Waheguru! Papa, Babaji & God, you know what I pray for, all my prayers, all my wishes, and I don't need to worry. Waheguru! Mere satguru tusi mehar karo. Papa, tusi mehar karo. Waheguru!

7/31/22

Papa? I just feel like the same person all these years, and so much has changed/happened. But I haven't changed. Papa, I miss 2020, when you were well, and I would message Daniel & he liked it. Papa, I miss everything before 2020, when all was fine & good. Papa, I was sure, and my dreams aligned. Papa, now I am not sure of anything or what I want. Papa, I leave it to you. Waheguru!

08/17/22

Papa, am I going forward or backward? Signed the contract at Plainview School for leave replacement. Called Reading Town in Syosset, and she needs a teacher, so that is all working out. Papa, I will miss the ESL kids at 167. Papa, I enjoyed connecting & learning about their culture.

Will miss speaking as much Spanish as I knew. Papa, at Plainview, those kids are going to be somewhat better off than the 167 kids. I enjoyed serving those 167 kids, and they would tell me to play Bad Bunny and talk about Columbia & their countries. Papa, I like that. I love different cultures, and it took me back to when I was in QC.

When I took Chinese cinema and Eastern European & Middle Eastern cinema, I loved being immersed in the culture and that world. Being exposed. The kids at 167 were good, but everyone else & everything else sucked. Papa, what can I do? She exceeded me, and 167 was a job. Not my cinema class or culture exposure opportunity. Perhaps that is the lesson. I need to fulfill that outlet through traveling & not ESL students.

Maybe I can do UNICEF teaching or Teachers without borders. Papa, I would like to have my own children & adopt. I want to help kids in need around the world. Papa, after 167, there might be a bigger role and a bigger road. As Oprah said, perhaps 167 was setting me up for something bigger/better. I just feel I was discriminated against by gender, race, and culture at 167. Gender because she is having Santiago & Chan do ESL. Racial because I am the only teacher of Indian descent. Cultural because they felt that since I don't know Spanish proficiently.

All their APs speak Spanish now. Papa, such a difference between men & women in work. Santiago is sorry but flirting & leaning into me. Papa, I can't work in Brooklyn and the Bronx, but it's too far. I don't want to do that commute. Papa, I can still serve kids & teach wherever I am. There are other dreams I need to fulfill, and perhaps that is why this happened, Papa. Waheguru!

9/3/22

Papa, I know you know that I did follow through and get the tenure. Morris wrote that she put it into the superintendent after Fekete told her. Papa, I had the narrative of getting the tenure & staying at 167, but Babaji & the universe have another plan for me, and I know I will be happy & it's best for me. It will align with what I want. Papa, look, the leave replacement got extended to Jan 30th from Dec. 6th. Papa, people wrote nice comments when I wrote a different past about starting at Roosevelt Elementary.

It goes to show, Papa, that Babaji has a bigger dream than you could have imagined. Babaji didn't want me to stay at 167, and I couldn't imagine a Plainview school job, but Babaji & God did. Morris needs to live with what she did and how she behaved, especially during the summer, with not getting back to me about the tenure. Papa, you know now what I want. You hear my prayers and wishes. Waheguru!

The tenure was me wanting validation for the injustice, or I made it for my father. My father came to my interview and demo lesson at the 167 school. I felt it would be a full close to get tenure and stay at 167 since my father saw me start there. Also, my first day as a teacher there was the same day as my father's birthday. Papa, this is for you and always was. The tenure did go through, but it just won't be activated since I don't have a permanent position at a DOE school, so I resigned and took what Babaji & God planned for me, which is Roosevelt.

"Today, I received tenure as a teacher. There were times when I thought this wouldn't happen. My father saw me and was beside me when I expressed doubt.

During that time, my father sternly said to stay strong and show them. After my dad passed, that is what I held on to. Also, prayer, hard work, and signs. I believe what is meant for you and where you are meant to be can't be interrupted. My first day at the school I teach in falls on the same day as my father's birthday.

I remember my dad coming with me to see the school and saying what a nice neighborhood. Dad, you are with me in all my classrooms. Reminding me to show them. I was happy when I got my first great observation but sad that I couldn't tell you how great it went. They say if you really want something with all your heart, then the entire universe works to help you get it. (Thanks to the support of great co-teachers, colleagues & students). Also, my mom, sisters, Jordan & Cole. Dad, you have a hand in this happening for me. I believe you will have a hand in everything I do. This is and was for you, Dad. We showed them! #tenured. Papa, I wouldn't

165

want to be in admin or supervisor. Rav is right; who wants to be responsible for someone's firing, removing, and giving bad reports/observations? To have that karma and be in your conscious. Yet, I did that in a way, and I am sorry. I do believe I got my karma in a way for that,

Waheguru!

167 chapter are closed, and new chapters have opened.

9/5/22

Encounters: Papa, Babaji & God, this is what my heart tells me. God is in our hearts. So this is what God & Babaji is telling my heart & me. Papa, I think of that line that God has already made the unions but has left us to meet/find the person (From Dil to Pagal Hai). God put Daniel and I in these settings, but we didn't meet or talk to each other. Papa & God will put us in a setting where it will be the right time to meet & talk to each other finally. Waheguru!

December 2019 at Brentt Park Holiday Market. Got pierogies and walked to the table where Sim & Rav were. Daniel was sitting at a table near with some guys.

He looked over, smiling as I was sitting like he liked that I was with my sisters. He was wearing a blue T-shirt with long hair. August 2020 at Central Park. I walked with Jordan, Rav & Daji. Daniel was on a Citi bike and stopped at a red light. He was wearing a white shirt, backward cap & neon sunglasses. He saw me crossing the street & I got a feeling to look at him. When I did, he was looking straight at me & then looked down to exhale. I was wearing a mask.

September 2020 at the Smith. I was waiting on the outside table with Jordan, Daji, Rav, Rashita & her boyfriend. Daniel came walking down the sidewalk smiling, and he was dressed up in a suit & messenger bag. He still had long, curly hair. He did notice me and smiled faintly but was still walking. I think that is why I fainted at

The Smith when I went with Laurie & Rav for brunch. I remembered.

December 2021 at Brentt Park Holiday Market. I was with Rav, Sim, and Cole. Jordan was with Daji at his apartment. We were walking through the stalls & Cole was in my LV bag. Rav was holding it like a box. Daniel was standing with glasses & white strands of hair. Not long curly but a slight blue bubble jacket. He saw me & Cole in a bag and then looked down. I looked at him & didn't have a mask on. I smiled, and a happy feeling came over & I said, "Waheguru." Thank you. Sean messaged me that morning.

Was it Daniel who hit on Rav by coming to our table in vandal on December 16, 2016? Rav & I were coming out of the bathroom. She was wearing a cut-out black dress. He was coming out of the bathroom, saw Rav & followed us to our table. He sat next to Rav & put his hand on her shoulder, smiling. I found him cute & handsome. But he was hitting on Rav & not me because I was wearing boots & jeans. Long sleeve shirt. He wasn't interested in me. Guys are jerks/evil like that, coming to a table to hit on someone but not caring how the others would feel, like me. Maybe I should have said "I am interested" to him.

9/25/22.

Papa, Ma said God & Babaji gave you a story from this when I told Ma that I started a screenplay about the things that happened to me at 167. Then, I said God & Babaji. Babaji has given me a lot of stories. Papa, I need to write them and deliver them to an audience. Papa, this is my purpose in my life, along with other things. I am not mad about leaving the DOE. Ma said a lot of nice things to me this evening. Ma asked me what was lacking in my life. She said how it is bad to have a job/place where you are relaxed and not pissed off like I was when I would wake up at 5 am for 167. Papa, that is family, care & love. People who notice a glow on your face and notice a change.

That is the love & family I grew up with, and that is what I wasn't used to: people who don't care & look out for you in the outside world. I remember writing I don't know how it feels not to have support. I told Ma that I feel God has written our lives & what comes is what is supposed to happen. There is no need to fear because it's mixed with love & joy.

9/27/22

Papa, Babaji, and God, it is time for you to deliver. I am grateful for everything I have, and I am lucky. I am grateful for my incredible family, who is my rock/support. For Jordan and our trips to Gurudwara & Trader's Joe for my job at Roosevelt Elem, which is 3 minutes away. I hit the jackpot with that and to be paid a salary & get benefits. Grateful for all the people I met at orientation who said you made the right decision. I am grateful for what I have now. But, I a ready for my partner and companion. My intuition, my dreams, and my signals to God aren't wrong. My prayers aren't wrong.

Daniel has a big family, and that is what I want. I always wanted that. Also, I want someone who will love and take care of me so I can focus on my writing/stories for an audience and have babies to raise. I am grateful for Roosevelt, but for all my years of teaching, I doubt building a career in teaching now. Especially since getting a partner, having babies, and writing my stories to an audience is more important to me than anything right now. Waheguru!

Papa, Babaji, and God, I know what you have planned for me, and what Papa, Babaji & God bring to me is best for me. Roosevelt is best because I can focus on myself and the other goals of my life. I will give my all & work hard at Roosevelt. Be competitive and driven as I can be, but I won't stress & chase. I have learned to leave work at work. Think ahead and move forward because I am where Papa, Babaji & God want me.

Waheguru, Waheguru, Waheguru!

Papa, Babaji & God, last night a dream with a lecture hall/space and the words Drexel University. A connection to Daniel. Papa, does this mean anything? I imagine meeting him at the Brentt Park Holiday Market finally. Papa, I want greatness. A life beyond horizons, I know. Papa, I want power, to be on top and leadership beside my companion. Papa, I remember everything. After taking a shower, you would go to the living room to do *paath*. Wouldn't get up and tell me to because you were doing *paath*. You're talkative at home and humorous. Being around you, Papa was completely at ease and had nothing to worry about. A world on our own and just simple. A world where I liked just being simple. A world where I liked just being your beti. Not everything was perfect. I remember when we would go out, and you would hold Cole near the window until we drove away. Papa, you are with me and with us. Waheguru! Papa, Babaji, and God, I want financial freedom for all of us.

10/3/22

Papa, Babaji & God, I want to move in with my boyfriend & partner after this leave replacement. I want to move in with Daniel Waheguru! Waheguru! Waheguru! Papa, Babaji & God, I believe all those people were Daniel. Marshall, who texted me when I went to the daisy farm with Sim, Rav, Jordan & Cole on August 13th. The speed dating with this guy was in May, and he texted me in August. I asked who he was because I didn't remember, and he said he was from speed dating. I wrote it's been a while since then. He wrote, "Why, are you dating someone." I wrote "No," and he asked what my summer had been. He wrote he had been going to the beach. He wrote if I lost the weight I said I gained during COVID. He wanted to know if I was dating someone & if I lost weight. Then was Jay from OKCupid, who wanted to do WhatsApp, but then he texted. This was during summer in the city.

He sounded like D, praising me for being a teacher and not wanting to talk on the phone. Then came Nate from Bumble. Papa, it sounded like Daniel. I don't think I am delirious here. He wrote how happy he was that the Giants won, and D had a story about how the Giants won. The texting at night & late at night, like Ethan, but also during the day. Nate talked on the phone during the day, but he said he was divorced with two kids in Garden City. He said he had just come back from Italy & London, and so did D.

When I told him why I texted him so late was due to Insomnia from back to school, he wrote, "Aww, you need a massage." I wrote, "Tea would help." Papa, it was when I fell and sprained my ankle. It was those convos where he said, can I move it like when you drive? Then he said it could be a hairline fracture that the x-ray couldn't show. You might need ortho, he said, and they have better X-rays with high definition. It sounded medical, and how does he, a finance guy, know this? He was at the U.S. Open after I claimed and Rav actually went to see Serena at night. I asked about his Bumble profile. He wrote he deleted it to detox. He texted me that night when I was in Green Gallow, and I wrote I was having dinner with friends in the city. Then he texted me the next night, and I wrote I was out in the city.

He asked where, and I wrote Chelsea when I was actually home, in bed with Jordan, because Rav went to pick Ma up from a party at midnight. He wrote, "Like on a date. Nice. So am I." I wrote "That's nice and enjoy." Papa, I asked to FaceTime twice, and he wrote, "Let's meet for a drink!" I wrote the last time that we have become text pen pals. He wrote he was thinking the same thing and let's meet for a drink/ I wrote that I wanted to FaceTime. He said "ok, how about tomorrow." And I wrote "ok." Papa, and that is where the halt and pause happened. Papa, Babaji & God, with all these people and Dr. Mark and convos. This is what I believe, and my intuition tells me. It is Daniel.

Papa, Babaji & God, I am proud of myself. Papa, I went to a Halloween party by myself in the city with a costume on. Papa, I can have fun, and I know once I meet my companion, my boyfriend, and my husband. I will have fun with him and with our children. Papa, I know. Waheguru, Waheguru, Waheguru!

11/8/22

Papa, I am proud of myself. Today was Parent Teacher Conferences at Roosevelt. I was working hard as I walked to multiple classrooms with folders and the laptop. I was confident while speaking to the parents. I realized what 167 gave me. It trained me so I know how to talk and parents to agree with my comments. I can work hard and start anew. Even though I am pulling out, I work more than Natalie & Elizabeth. I am proving it to myself. I can say my white counterparts, but then I am saying Asians or minorities have to work harder or are given more work than non-minorities. Thinking that way isn't going to help me in any way. I won't assimilate if I think that way. So, I won't. Waheguru, Waheguru, Waheguru! Then I worked in RT for 3 hours (4-7 pm). Waheguru!

11/15/22

Papa, Babaji & God, yesterday I found out I was positive for COVID.

Papa, we know you are watching over us and protecting us. Papa, I don't know why I panicked when driving to get my hair done by Margaretann. I got to the salon, and I felt I was going to faint. Papa, I am not proud of what I have become. This fear and being scared. Even at the dentist's yesterday and nervous around the Markoff Whitestone today, it was the trauma of the 167. It just reminds me of when I wouldn't go into Rite Aid after getting into a fight with the manager & quitting. I am still sensitive, and I don't want to be. Leaving 167 or being excessed was good. I needed to leave there, and the universe removed me for my good. I shouldn't be scared to drive to Whitestone. What should have been a fun & relaxing afternoon wasn't. I am disappointed that I did that. It's okay because we have bad days. Waheguru, Waheguru, Waheguru!

1/1/23

Papa, Happy New Year! Papa, Ma and I went to Sant Sagar Gurdwara on Thursday evening for your langar. I drove Ma in my new car (Mercedes). I wore the light blue jacket that I wore to the funeral and paath. Papa, being in Sant Sagar Gurdwara was powerful because Ma & I felt your energy, spirit, and presence. The minute we stepped into the Gurudwara, it was going back into a time capsule. I was back in that time/world when you were with us, Papa. I would be with you and Ma in any familiar setting, and you would be walking around.

Even if you were out of my sight, Papa, when you walked towards me, I felt your energy. When Ma & I were eating langar downstairs, Ma started crying. One of the priests asked me to show a picture of you, and he remembered who you were. He said, "So fit and active." When I sat to listen to Kirtan and from all those YouTube videos we saw of you sitting at Sant Sagar, listening, I would look in the direction of the men's side of the Darbar Hall and know where you usually sat. Papa, I felt your energy, and it felt like you were sitting listening to Kirtan. Papa, it was powerful, and I started tearing up. I like that feeling, Papa. The feeling of being connected to something bigger & powerful than anything that is here & now. Papa, that was Queens, and that year of 2020, and after moving to Plainview, I felt so connected to Babaji, God, and their spirits/voices.

When I was walking to take Mata at Sant Sagar, I was walking the same steps & paths as you, Papa, watching you walk down and take Mata. Watching you give money to the ragis and I did the same that evening. That is love, family, and legacy. To honor you, Papa, by doing the things you did that gave you peace & joy. The love never dies; it continues back & forth. When Ma and I left the gurdwara, it was like leaving Queens and the feelings of the world where you were with us, Papa, in the physical sense.

I got into the car, Papa, and in front, I saw an MD sign on the license plate of the car. Papa, I said, "Waheguru." When I went to the holiday shaka party, I went to get pizza near Penn Station afterward.

I was walking, and an ambulance from Mount Sinai went past me. Papa, Babaji, and God, only you know what that means; if it means anything, Papa, you are communicating with us all, and I don't need to worry because you are watching over us and protecting us. This morning, you would ask, "How was the party?" But after saying, "Harleen, Happy New Year!" I know your energy, voice, and spirit, Papa. It lives on, Papa. You live on. Waheguru! Waheguru! Waheguru!

Papa, I am late with writing. It's been busy. Rav got the driveway done, and at night, I parked my black Mercedes next to Rav's white Mercedes. Rav looked out from the front window and said, "Dono cars ache tara fit age, space hai." At that moment, Rav looked and sounded just like you, Papa. The way she was looking out. I even told Rav and Ma. Papa, Rav said our lives had changed when I got the Mercedes. She was referring to all we saw & went through with cars as a family. The timeline of cars gets me upset & angry. To think of all the struggles & losses we saw. The best example is one day, the electricity would be cut, and when that came back, we realized the cable was cut. Papa, I know everyone goes through hardships.

With the Mercedes, I think back to how, in high school, I saw the Mitishbushi Eclipse with LD lights in the condo across the street. They were Korean, and I expressed to Sim how I wanted that car. Never thought I would have a Mercedes, and it has ambient lights. Never thought I would walk around and run around Penn Station to find Track 18. I looked at one side, and then I turned to the other side to find it there. Papa,

I eat the pizza near Penn Station and always do it with Rav or Sim. Doing it on my own. I had a dream of the words Jupiter and the Oscars. I had my third observation, and I was calm. Another thing, I didn't think I would teach in Long Island. Papa, they say God & Babaji dream a bigger dream for you. But I don't think it's just that. Papa, you are with Babaji, and you have your dreams for us, dreams for yourself, and you saw how perhaps we were stuck and accepting what was due to situations. Papa, your love, your legacy as our father, husband, & grandfather is to see to it that we fulfill your dreams & ours. Waheguru! Waheguru! Waheguru!

Papa, even though you didn't move into this house with us, I know how you would carry about around the house. I know where you would sit to watch TV. How you would walk around the kitchen and how you would sound, Papa. I think of the memories, but it feels like it was yesterday. Rav said it should feel that way because it's only been two years. (Natalie said it's still fresh). Papa, I want it to always feel like yesterday. I don't want to forget. I want to remember everything. Waheguru.

Papa, thinking a lot about you this evening. I was driving from RT, and I thought of your giggle/laugh, like a flashback of when you got these Hispanic guys to reupholster the sofa in the condo. They were leaving and I heard from my room you saying he is a good worker because a new guy came the second day. Papa, I know the exact tone and giggle after. I wish I could go back to those times of being in the condo. Ma said you can't go back, but just forward. Papa, I haven't forgotten any of those moments in the condo. It's still fresh when I remember.

Papa, I don't ever want to forget those beautiful moments. They are my stories and part of my legacy. Waheguru. Papa, Babaji & God, what you have planned for me, just give it now & present it. Where you want me, place me now. Who you want me with and around, bring now. Papa, I don't want to wonder anymore. Especially since he came in my dream, I saw an ambulance with the words Mount Sinai when I went to Shaka wine tasting on Wednesday. Waheguru!

Papa, Babaji & God, I was thinking about what you once said to me in the kitchen of the condo or triplex. Oh no! I don't remember where. Papa, you said, "Find someone on your own, Harleen!" I was taken aback. I also didn't have the guts to do that. Papa, there was awhile until last night that I wished I had the guts then. Papa, I would have found someone, and you would have met him. Papa, that is wrong for me to feel.

You wouldn't want me to do that to myself. Papa, I have the guts now, Papa, and you are in a place where you can guide me to him. Papa, there is a lot of work to be still done. I can't be in a place of anger and all that happened is how it was to be. I will love and be intimate with a man who wants me and opens his life to me. We will have babies, and I will write my stories. That is the fairness, and you will know him, Papa, because you are watching & helped bring him to me. He, my babies, and my stories are an extension of your love, Papa. Papa, I don't care about the teaching. It's just a job and paycheck. Him, my babies, my stories, and my family are all I want, Papa. Waheguru, Waheguru, Waheguru!

Papa, Babaji & God, free me so I can live and do my purpose. Allow me to do my purpose. That Sunday, when I was emotional, Rav said I used to be someone who gave good advice. Rav asked me what happened to that person. She said I don't know what happened to that person. I texted Sim, and she said you got hung over stupid things, and you lost your clarity. She also added that it was when I was working at the middle school. Then I remembered the things I said pre-2016, and Rav would come from Geico, & I would know she was upset and say uplifting things.

I remember saying to Sim when she was driving that when you get things early, that's not good, but when you get things with struggle, then that's worth it. Papa, Babaji & God, I liked being that person. Morris said you have to want it (tenure & teaching). Then I think my Rogue got hit so that I won't have a car payment & job necessities, and I can focus on my writing & stories. Papa, Babaji & God, I was trying to be someone else and chasing another life. Papa, Babaji & God, you did free me from 167.

That place wasn't doing me well, and it made me lose myself, try to be someone else, and chase another life. Papa, Babaji & God, all I ask is that you let me fulfill my purpose, and I know part of that is writing the stories. I have taken screenwriting courses, and I know what to do, but I just can't get myself situated to write from a good or authentic place. I am writing about experiences at 167 during 2020 & D, which I think is stupid writing/self-centered writing. I want the writing to be aligned with my purpose, my talent, and my creativity, and people will respond to it. Papa, Babaji & God, let me do my purpose, let my mind be clear, and not get stuck & hung up on things that don't serve my purpose and be in service always. Waheguru! Waheguru! Waheguru!

4/12/23

Papa, Babaji, & God, Nuvpreet, Gurvir, and their kids came on Easter Sunday. They stayed until 1 am, and I remember how one evening you just went to bed when they were here. I asked if you were sleeping, and you said they were okay with it.

Rav was talking about how she went to the medium and he knew the connection you had with Rav. She was your go-to person, and that is why Papa wrote Rav's cell number on the paper when coming off the ventilator. Ma was telling them about driving everywhere because we only had one car.

Rav said to them how Papa said life & death weren't up to us when Vicki passed, and she said the men in Papa's family passed young. I though about the one car and how when it was hot, we would not sit in the car when waiting for Ma. Rav & Ma were saying nice things, and I was initially angry because their kids went to 167. And I find MY anger very interesting that a connection was still built towards that place, and I couldn't say things about those teachers. Papa, I just feel the world sucks and people are mean/selfish. But 167 is not the world. Perhaps it's just the teaching field. Papa, I made a complaint against Natalie at Roosevelt. Papa, I don't know if I ruined my chances of getting a job there or in the district. Papa, she was being mean, and I couldn't take it. Papa, I stood up for myself, and I don't regret that.

Papa, I don't know where I will be in September with regard to my job. I know you know Papa, and that comforts me because I know you will take care of me and are. Papa, I don't know if I am being bared to the purpose of writing. Sim was upset that the CPS letter had her name. Rav brought up the petition having her name and she was a lawyer. She wnet to that court & the landlady of the triplex sent that. Papa, so many experiences, but that is life, and that applies to everyone. Waheguru!

I think of Nuvpreet and remember Ma said she wanted Sim to marry him but he was interested in Rav. Even though Nuvpreet didn't marry into our family, he became a close family member & his family has been with us all these years. Ma told Nuvpreet about a dream where Dhaji took Ma to a room where Pa was, and Papa was so happy and said to Ma I am good and happy. Nuvpreet said that's what you should remember and keep in mind. He also said whoever is on her mind comes to our dream. He has also assured me that the city schools are overpopulated. It's more work, and you are close to home.

Papa, Babaji, & God, on Saturday, I found out D got engaged. Papa, the pattern continued and that upsets me, Papa. Why did I make this guy a focus for 3 years? Papa, what I find unfair is that they were growing or developing a relationship, and I couldn't. Instead, I went through painful experiences. Papa, if D was interested in the beginning of 2020, and I was dating him, then the timing wasn't good. After 2020, I was healing & grieving, yet time was moving & they were growing in their relationship.

While sort of healed, then another thing (excessed). Papa, perhaps this is a good closure. To close all these traumatic things that happened. A fresh start. D was the outlet to escape & not think about the crappy job I was at, many people, and all that occurred in 2020. Papa, I believe I am where I am supposed to be, and I am happy. I am not looking for something as an outlet to escape anything. I don't know what those signs, messages, and dreams were. I do believe that place & those people were crappy due to how they responded twice to unfortunate things that happened to me. They weren't human or couldn't be. I guess that is the boundaries (crossing the street to my car & Fabrizio & Jensen looking at me). Some were nice. Papa, it's in the past, and looking at the girl in a bikini walking around a beach & him.

They don't look anything great. They look trashy and not classy. Perhaps that aligns with where I was at the time (JHS 167). A job is a job, and it doesn't align with who you are or your personal life. Papa, I am ready to meet my companion and partner. Papa, I am ready for all the blessings because I have done the work, and I am in peace/content. I went through what I had to get here and where I am. 167 gave me the experience, and so did life. Natalie Carrol asked me about Husan & I know what I am doing. Waheguru!

Papa, what happened? Cole passed away yesterday morning. MA, Rav & I stood at LIVS as Cole was lying on the table with tubes, and the nurse was pumping oxygen into him. The two doctors came in and looked straight at us in the eyes. It was all clear. He was gone and just on machines. As the doctor was talking, and said there is limited brain function. We are talking and saying, "So," then sobbing because we know. We said our goodbyes and went to the parking lot. They called and said Cole had passed. It was literally 20 minutes after they stopped pumping. They called Sim because Rav was in her car with Ma doing a deposition. We went back into LIVS, and we held Cole in a room. He was wrapped in a green blanket. For me, it's just this used to death. Papa, I had an instinct, just like I had about you, Papa. I am sorry, but I saw my wedding without you, and I think without Cole. If my instinct is correct, then my instinct about Daniel should be correct. Papa, these past 3 years and two deaths. We don't want this, Papa. Cole was our family member, and he was there when you were there. Now, our family is smaller, and I don't understand why. Papa, you really loved Cole, and perhaps you wanted Cole.

There has to be a reason. Maybe you weren't happy with how Cole was being taken care of, so you called him to take care of him. Perhaps you saw too much juggling, or maybe Papa, and you really want us to find our companions/partners and have babies. Have our families and new members come to the club and not carry on with just memories of the past or hold on to the club that was. Papa, life experiences, and with Cole, we were prepared because we have been through this road. We didn't put him on the ventilator because we knew we had to let him go in peace. It was quick, and he didn't suffer. I prayed for him to come home, like I did for you, Papa. This was Babaji and God's will. Thank you, Cole, for the love. I want to share my stories, Babaji. Waheguru!

Papa, I really want answers. Papa, ask Babaji and God and give me answers. Papa, I finished the leave replacement, and I threw out all the stuff I brought there from Whitestone. I didn't want to carry that stuff. I didn't see a purpose. If I am meant to teach, then I will teach and get the stuff I need. Papa, I don't want to think about the teaching and make some meaning behind throwing out the stuff. I learned job is a job, and I don't take it personally. Papa, I want my companion, my soul mate, my man. Papa, I am attracted to D, to Dr. Mark and even to Evan from OKC.

I imagine kissing them, and for me, they are charming. Papa, I want that, and what is wrong with that? Maybe I can find Evan again on OKC. I enjoyed that time, and now it's fallen flat. Papa, D is still resonated in me and if I am immature, childish, or 15, then I am. Papa, I still have hope, and I don't know if that is wrong to believe. When D came into my dreams, it felt good because it kept me hopeful. Papa, that is why I need answers. Waheguru!

Papa, I have to say that times do heal somewhat. I am not angry anymore about the LHS 167 experience and don't hold resentment. It is partly also due to the Roosevelt experience. I got all good/effective observations. My summative score from the principal was highly effective. Now, the question is if I still want to teach. Despite good observations, do I love it, and can I sustain it? Well, if I want a livelihood and salary then yes, why did I leave angry on the last day, because I felt that it wasn't fair that I didn't have a job offer. After all the hard work and knowing I am a more qualified/good teacher. Papa, I have to leave it up to God and Babaji. You know, Papa. Waheguru! Waheguru! Waheguru!

7/7/23

Papa, I took Jordan to I Hop for breakfast this morning. That name became audible because the manager came in to check everything. The manager's name was Daniel. Every step with me in becoming a teacher. I believe I rose to what you told me. To be strong and show them. You dropped me to schools so I can teach, you would want me to be happy, Papa. You also told someone that I was going to go to Hollywood. Papa, you were with me as I did these jobs. I never felt alone. You would encourage me to my passion, just like Ma says, Papa, you would say to be logical and happy. You made everything I did sound great. You left it to me to make my decisions.

Papa, I know you are watching. Jordan & Raveena, please lessen Rav's stress, Papa. Waheguru, Waheguru & Waheguru! Papa, the therapist Joem said it was noble that after some time, I am talking about you and wanting to honor you by writing your story and our stories. Waheguru, Waheguru, Waheguru. When you want something, when you put something out there, and it comes from a place of want, then it can't be denied. When I put out the website for teacher tenure, it didn't come from a place of want. When I decided to write this book, I wanted an audience to hear my Papa's stories. When I put my stories out there, they will be embraced. Waheguru!

7/24/23

Papa, please make something great come from the journal entries that I sent to Amazon Publishing. Papa, I didn't want to write another entry here since submitting the entries. However, I was thinking as I was on the treadmill at another gym. I was thinking my stories are all I have left, Papa. Papa, I have tried everything to sustain something and spark something. I tried to sustain my teaching career.

182

I tried to spark a relationship. It didn't go my way, and here I am, not upset or pleading, but saying all I want is their stories, my stories, to go somewhere. Papa, I know from my experience that Babaji and God have always given me what I need and not want. Papa, I need my stories and Amazon Publishing to go somewhere. Papa, I think the unemployment would be best. I can't see myself teaching in a school. I don't think I have any more to give to this with all I have been through. Papa, to have the time to continue working on being my best self.

Papa, I want a fit body, a bikini, work on writing and books with Amazon and be with my companion. Papa, that is the life I want, and I guess I knew that a while back. Papa, I don't know what is best for me right now. Papa, guide me to my best so I can be happy and help Rav, Ma, Jordan and Andy. That would be the best. Waheguru, Waheguru, Waheguru!

8/19/23

Rav had pre-season tickets for the Jets from her firm. As Rav was driving to Met Stadium in New Jersey, she mentioned how this was the route she took Papa on when going to the hospital in Manhattan. It was the summer of 2020 and Rav was saying that when they got there, Papa was having anxiety since there was a hill. Papa said he couldn't walk up the hill to NY Presbetarian Hospital, and Papa was having a hard time.

There was a bench, and Papa sat on it. And Rav gave Papa a pep talk to not turn back and go home. At that time, we thought Papa was just having anxiety, but it was Papa's lungs. He was having a hard time breathing, and we heard him wheezing at times. That is why he couldn't walk too much, want to drive or eat the meals we cooked Papa. As Rav and I were talking about this, I felt guilty. I should have taken Papa to the hospital, but he wouldn't have gone with me. Papa trusted Rav, and she was his go-to person. During that time (2020), I said to Papa that I could take you, and he said, "No, Rav will take me, and that is better."

I feel guilty that I should have stepped up to be the go-to person as well. I was 35 years old at that time. Yet, I was consumed with my life and wanted to have my companion. Rav said that dreams have an expiration date and she is reminded of that from that hospital experience. She felt Papa shouldn't have gone to the city on the subway at 70 years old, but he did because of Mom. She wanted him to make all this money.

I just remember how Rav and I decided to get a family cell phone plan. We asked Ma and Papa to join the plan. They would get new cell phones, and at that time, Papa had a free cell phone plan under his insurance. I told Papa to call them and tell them you don't need that plan and to release your cell number so you can still use it. I heard Papa talking to them on the phone, and they were asking why they were leaving the plan. They were trying to get Papa to stay. Papa was amused and said I am joining a family plan and don't need this plan anymore. As adults we have so many conversations with people to not take us out of the plan or service, so it is humorous when someone is trying to get you to stay.

08/24/23

Papa, Babaji, & God, yesterday Manav's grandmother came to visit Ma at the house. After all the years and everything, I felt less around her, for the messages I sent and the one Manav sent me about harassment and wanting me to call him so we can discuss it. Yesterday, when she came, it took me back to that time and that not good person I became & can be when I feel hopeless. They and the others saw the worst version of me. I feel foolish and guilty that I did something so pathetic. I have these messages in the archive on FB. The one Manav sent me in 2016 about the messages I sent. It makes me feel so small and that I don't deserve anything, so why ask?

Manav works in 7-11, and Ma, Rav, & Sim asked would want to be with someone like that. Someone who takes handouts money from the in-laws. I just feel so less due to how I have behaved that who am I to judge anyone? Manav and his family wanted the woman who has rich parents, to take hand-outs.

Then, I would never fit the equation since I don't have that source. British psychic had said I should feel lucky that I got to see what became of these guys since a lot don't get that. He works in 7-11 in Margaretland, and she works an office job. His dream when he got married was that his father-in-law would set him up in his business. She finished medical school when she got married and wanted to do a residency to become a doctor. Both of their dreams got crushed and yet they were married.

Now they have two kids. I don't still want him, but I wish that there was some tangible progress in my life, so that yesterday it didn't seem like I am still in the same place. Last time, that woman said to Ma that she should make her status. I can't help to feel that she sees us as less. Waheguru, Waheguru, Waheguru.

8/31/23

Papa, Babaji, and God, I have to be able to look at him & the female (her) and say I will have that too. I will be in Italy with my person too. As Rav said, but is going to Italy that important? Is that everything, Papa? I am giving power to people who are just common & ordinary people. Papa, I have to believe there are wonderful things for me. Papa, Babaji, & God have things planned for me that I could never imagined, and it will surprise me to the core. That is why I shouldn't cry or be angry about 167, Roosevelt, or getting unemployment & working in RT again. Papa, Babaji, & God, this is what is written & the plan for me right now. I have to embrace it and be the best. In the past three years, there was a lot that happened.

I was angry, grieving, and sad because I thought you weren't on my side, Babaji & God, because you took Papa, my job at 167, My Nissan Rogue, and Cole. It wasn't like you didn't give. Babaji and God, you gave me a bigger house to live in, a job at Roosevelt school, which was 4 minutes away, and a new Mercedes car, which is a first for me and Andy, the puppy. Yet I couldn't see it that way because I wanted you to give me that one person. Babaji and God, I feel I am somewhat healed and have grieved since I don't question that you aren't on my side. I am mellow now and not sad or angry about all that has happened in the past three years. I take Mami to her doctor's appointments and drop her off at her parties/events.

I am okay with that now, since before, I was upset and felt it unfair how my life has changed and the responsibilities now. I wish Papa were here and, not because he can do all the things he did for Mami & the family, but so he can see how we have progressed. But I know we are because of Papa being near Babaji. Papa is powerful and I know he is watching and doing for us. Waheguru, Waheguru, Waheguru!

9/5/23

Papa, Babaji & God, on Sunday, I drove to Long Island City, parked my car on the street, and walked to the pool party. Papa, something I never did before and never thought I could do, I did. When I got into the car and drove home, I said thank you, Papa, for helping me do this. Papa, yesterday Gurvir came, and I got angry. She said 167 has 6 postings for para and one teacher. She was saying Veer is in honors, and it sounded like 167 is this great place with great teachers. Today was Roosevelt's first day and I saw those faces I worked with. Papa, I couldn't set myself in 167 or set in Roosevelt, and I am bitter since I have no standing, but I know these aren't the only places in the world. I went to New Hyde Park RT and I went to the Rite Aid first.

I was angry since I blamed Ma for bringing Gurvir over. Then the honeybee song played after I rudely asked the pharmacist where is the Allegra. The song made me smile and put me in a happy mood. It was the song D had on a video for some contest. Then I saw Mr. Song & Mrs.Song. They were nice. He shook my hand when I was walking to RT from Rite Aid, and she recognized me and said my name. Then told the RT manager that I worked in Little Neck and that I am a very experienced RT teacher. There is the standing. Papa, Babaji & God, I know there is a reason why I am where I am. I can't be angry like Rav said. I am collecting unemployment until mid-January. There is nothing to be ashamed of. I need to embrace this time and enjoy/make the most/best of it. Rav said when you will get this time again. Waheguru, Waheguru, Waheguru!

9/24/23

Papa, I feel you are even more powerful and able to help me & us more on the other side. It's what an astrologer said, but she tapped on what I already felt/thought. Papa, you are helping me every step of the way. I have been asking you, Papa, with regards to what would be the better place. The part-time position at Massapequa with RT in the afternoon or full-time at DOE Bleeker. Wednesday evening, I got a supplement check from DOE and I had gotten one in February. I feel it's you, Papa. Sim said everything evens out in the end. Everything comes full circle.

With all the things we had to pay for. I think of the Chase Disney Credit card that was opened by my parents and used for their business without me knowing. Now, here are these DOE checks that came, and I don't know why. People said just take it and enjoy. Great things are coming Rav's way with job offers. Babaji, God, & Papa, I am grateful for the two job offers. Papa, you are taking care of things. Waheguru, Waheguru! Papa, Babaji, & God, working at Bleeker & Doe gives me health benefits with a full salary. I can freeze my eggs,

Papa, and pay for what insurance won't cover. Papa, I want to have kids. I want to know what being pregnant feels like. Papa, I want to have more than one kid and be pregnant more than once. I want to have a big family, Papa. Papa, I leave it to you to give me a sign and answer on what is the best place to work. Waheguru, Waheguru, Waheguru!

10/20/23

Papa, Babaji, & God, Bleeker's position fell through, and that is your answer when I asked for clarity. I looked at your picture, Papa and Babaji while asking where I should work. Papa, you were saying what my intuition was saying, Massapequa. Even when I picked from two papers, it came up Massapequa. This is not bad, and it's not that no one wants me to freeze my eggs or have babies. Papa, I have to close the DOE chapter and move on because the move on is better.

The move-on doesn't make me feel bad or less. It makes me feel hopeful. The move-on doesn't remind me of all the let-downs, falls, and disappointments. As of yesterday morning, the paperwork for DOE was still processing then the principal called. It is true that what is meant for you can't be taken from you. What is meant for you falls into place in an instant.

Everything falls into place, and that is how you know it's right. When you let go of something that isn't right for you or even the idea of having/getting something that doesn't feel right, you feel free, and you exhale that sigh of relief. Thank you for that, Papa, Babaji, & God, thank you for saving me from getting into something that isn't right for me. Waheguru, Waheguru, Waheguru! It's a good thing I took the job at Massapequa. Follow your intuition ♥.

It saved me; I took the Massapequa job, and the DOE paperwork was never processed completely, and the principal withdrew the nomination/position due to enrolment & their data.

188

The truth is the ENL kids aren't all going to get serviced, and they will get away with it. That is the DOE or Department of Education. When I told, I was excessed and had to come to JHS 167. I was anxious, and I went into Katsoras's office and I told her I was getting anxious. She said you need motivation to get through, and she said, "What is meant for you can't be taken from you."

What happened with Bleeker is not just the universe and Papa closing the DOE door for me, but there was a lesson. I felt me being excessed from JHS 167 was part that I was a minority in that building. I felt if I was white/Caucasian, then Morris wouldn't have excessed me, and that is what I told the District Union Representative.

Bleeker offered me a position and took it away. However, the principal and assistant principal were not white but Asian-American. They probably knew what happened to me because I worked with them that summer after I was excessed. They probably knew because people talk. So they called me for an interview, and both Patricia and Mr. Leung greeted me warmly with respect. They remembered me from the summer in the city. It is a reflection that it's a nice building with nice people. I feel that the $800 supplement after I accepted the position was the universe, and Papa knew that the job would fall through. So here is the money/wages for my loss and damages.

Why the paperwork was never processed, was the universe and Papa. This door is not meant to open again. Or am I coded since I didn't give a 30-day notice when I resigned? However, HR connected and said it didn't matter. DOE is such a disorganized and mismanaged mess.

Epilogue

I am responsible, and no one else. After I got excessed from LHS 167, if I didn't want the disturbance in my benefits and paycheck, then I should have just stayed in the school they placed me in, or the one Morris told me about in Union Street. However, I chose to resign from the DOE and take the leave replacement position, knowing it wasn't permanent. If I stayed, I wouldn't have broken into hives in the summer or recently when the unemployment stopped. I am responsible. I was responsible when I chose to request Daniel on Instagram when I didn't get a response on Tinder. I am responsible for messaging him and liking his comments when he doesn't initiate a conversation. I am responsible for getting my emotions invested in him when he didn't ask for my number or like me back on Tinder.

I am responsible for how I react and my actions. I was responsible for getting upset when he didn't like me back. I am responsible for the things I did because he didn't do anything to me. This is not a toy store where I didn't get the toy, so that person is wrong, and they need to say sorry to me. I am responsible for my life, to fix it and make it one where I am happy. To do that, I have to let go of everything that has happened. I have to let go of all the bad things that came as a domino effect these past three years. Morris told me she couldn't nominate me for tenure or an extension and, therefore, I wouldn't be back in September of 2020.

Papa suddenly and unexpectedly getting sick, the pandemic with schools shutting down, Papa passing away, getting excessed, getting COVID, my car getting hit on Thanksgiving, dealing with the newly divorced Natalie in Pasadena, Cole unexpectedly dislocating his neck and passing away after fusion surgery, the leave replacement ending and not getting a job offer at the district, ending up with no paycheck in the summer and having to work in RT, going on unemployment, having to work in RT Syosset and New Hyde Park.

However, good things did happen. Raveena bought a home in Plainview. For one year, I got to work four minutes from home, and I made more money than before; I got a Mercedes, I submitted my journal entries to Amazon Publishing, I learned how to save money, and I got a part-time job at Massapequa High School. One thing I am most grateful for is the support of my family, and I felt so connected to you, Babaji, and God. I still feel connected to you, Papa. After you passed away, it was a different connection that I never experienced before.

Only those who lose a loved one experience it, and it was to my surprise. It was to my surprise, and I didn't expect to ever go through a feeling like that or an experience like that. It changes you forever. My intuition was really strong at that time and my connection to something bigger than myself. I needed that to get through that time when you had just passed, Papa.

I didn't mention or write the name Daniel here. What is there to write? Was it a negative or a positive? I created it, and I don't know if those dreams or the guy on the bike I saw was really him in the summer of 2020 or if I wanted it to be him. Was I just creating that? Perhaps that was how I coped or my coping mechanism during 2020 and after. When things were happening in the home that were too intense, I wrote. Yet this time, I wasn't writing made-up stories and characters on paper. I was creating with my own life.

Where I was the character, and Daniel was the character. I never was able to write love stories as a screenplay, but I did with my own life during that time. Thinking that some of the people I conversed with on the apps via text or phone were him disguised. Especially the ones that said they were doctors. So that is that. This is now part of my journey. It continues, but also part of my past that I need to make peace with and learn from so that I don't behave that way again or go down that track of thought. Learn and let go, but how can I let go of Papa? How that world was and felt like when Papa was here. It is something I don't want to forget.

However, I think, being how I was in that world, was someone who wasn't responsible and didn't know how to cope when not getting the toy and turning to create. Papa's love kept me as the little girl and the youngest. There is no shame in that, and it's part of my growth. Papa was to be in my presence to hear and see for only 36 years of my life, but Papa is by my side forever. Yes, I can be angry with just 36 years and him not seeing me fall in love (except for those crushes), get married, have kids, write, publish, and so much more, or I can find comfort with the forever.

When Papa was here, he worked really hard. He took the public bus and NYC subway to work despite the weather. He wasn't calculative or an aggressor. He just worked hard, and that is what I keep in mind. I take the train and subway to teach at a new school. As I walk down to the subway platform, I am aware that my father did this. His presence is one that I can feel and see. No one knows what "more" is for anyone when we are here. It really is about loving what you do get to see.

My father saw success, but he also saw many setbacks which tested his esteem. My father was loved, and he knew that when he went out into the world. I know I am loved also, but looking for more love. Papa and I never talked about "more." Yet I believe Papa being on my side now means that "more" is for me. It's not an illusion but can be a reality.

www.ingramcontent.com/pod-product-compliance
Lightning Source LLC
Chambersburg PA
CBHW051514120626
46551CB00012B/912